A writer and editor, Laurence Fenton lives in Cork. His work centres upon the social and political history of nineteenth-century Ireland and Britain.

FREDERICK DOUGLASS
IN IRELAND

In the summer of 1845, a man named Frederick Douglass disembarked ship in Dublin. It marked the start of a two-year lecture tour of Britain and Ireland by the celebrated author, orator — and escaped slave. Advised to leave America for his own safety after the publication of his eloquent and incendiary abolitionist memoir, Douglass proceeded to spend four months in Ireland describing and denouncing the horrors of slavery: packing full halls with his oratorical skill; sharing a stage with 'The Liberator' Daniel O'Connell; and taking the pledge from 'The Apostle of Temperance' Fr. Theobald Mathew.

LAURENCE FENTON

FREDERICK DOUGLASS IN IRELAND

'The Black O'Connell'

Complete and Unabridged

ULVERSCROFT
Leicester

First published in Great Britain in 2014 by
The Collins Press
Cork

First Large Print Edition
published 2015
by arrangement with
The Collins Press
Cork

A catalogue record for this book is available
from the British Library.

ISBN 978–1–4448–2543–5

Published by
F. A. Thorpe (Publishing)
Anstey, Leicestershire

Set by Words & Graphics Ltd.
Anstey, Leicestershire
Printed and bound in Great Britain by
T. J. International Ltd., Padstow, Cornwall

This book is printed on acid-free paper

For Katherine

Contents

Prologue

Baltimore, USA — c. 1830

The young slave approached the Irishmen unbidden. They were unloading stones from a scow, a small vessel used for transporting cargo to and from ships lying in harbour. It was heavy work, but the boy, no more than twelve or thirteen years old, was quick to help. He was a powerful youth and clearly familiar with the world of the docks. When they finished, one of the men asked the boy if he was a slave. 'I told him I was. He asked, 'Are ye a slave for life?' I told him that I was. The good Irishman seemed to be deeply affected by the statement. He said to the other that it was a pity so fine a little fellow as myself should be a slave for life. He said it was a shame to hold me.' The Irishmen told him to escape north. He would find friends there and be free. The boy feigned ignorance. 'White men,' he wrote later, had 'been known to encourage slaves to escape, and then, to get the reward, catch them and return them to their masters.' Nevertheless, the boy remembered the advice, resolving from that time to run away.

Baltimore, on whose harbour this brief meeting took place, was one of the largest and most important cities in America, shipping grain from the Midwest and cotton from the South all over the world. It was a crush of canneries, factories, warehouses, mills and shipbuilding yards, dubbed 'The Monumental City' by President John Quincy Adams on account of its surfeit of churches and statues. It was also the gateway to America for many thousands of European immigrants, mainly Irish and German, second only to Ellis Island in New York. The two Irishmen unloading the scow were deeply representative of the immigrant experience, escaping poverty and/or persecution at home for a life of hard labour in the burgeoning metropolises of the United States.

The young slave lending them a hand was Frederick Bailey, better known to the world as Frederick Douglass.

1

Masters and Slaves

Frederick Douglass was never sure of his age. A majority of masters kept such precious, deeply personal information away from their slaves. It was a sign of power, one manifestation of the many iniquities of slavery. Frederick's best guess was February 1817. He was out by a year — the real date fell somewhere in February 1818. The uncertainty hurt even as a child: 'The white children could tell their ages. I could not tell why I ought to be deprived of the same privilege.' Frederick's sense of place was far more secure: born in Talbot County, Maryland, the latest in a long-established line of Talbot County slaves, one that stretched back to the early years of the colony.

Frederick's first years were spent in a cabin by a creek on the rural Eastern Shore of Chesapeake Bay. He lived with his grandparents, Isaac and Betsey Bailey, and an ever-changing collection of siblings and cousins. It was a cramped and basic shelter, with windowless log walls and some planks

3

thrown over the rafters to act as beds. Frederick's clothes were few and the food, despite his grandmother's best efforts, was often of the 'coarsest kind', cornmeal mush picked off a wooden tray with an oyster shell. And yet Frederick's memories of this time were positively bucolic, the many hardships leavened by the thrill of being a child in the warm countryside, running wild through the trees, rolling in the dust and plunging head-first into the muddy waters of the Tuckahoe Creek.

Frederick's father was a white man, quite possibly his owner Aaron Anthony, a farmer in his fifties who was also estate manager at the nearby plantation, Wye House. His skin colour, certainly, was of a far lighter hue than the rest of his family. Frederick's mother, Harriet Bailey, lived and worked on one of Anthony's farms a few miles away (Anthony owned about thirty slaves, spread over a couple of farms). He saw her rarely, for although the distance between them was not great, it was almost impossible for field-hands to leave their place of work. 'The slave-mother', Frederick wrote angrily in later years, 'can be spared long enough from the field to endure all the bitterness of a mother's anguish, when it adds another name to a master's ledger, but *not* long enough to receive the joyous reward afforded by the intelligent smiles of her child.' Harriet died quite young, when Frederick was six or seven years old, and the pain of never really knowing her was a source of lifelong grief.

Cut off from his mother, the greatest influence on Frederick's early years was his grandmother Betsey. It appears that Betsey, about forty-four years old when Frederick was born, was left to look after the children so that the mothers — her daughters — could be put back to work in the fields as soon as possible after giving birth. She was illiterate, like the majority of slaves, but quite skilled at providing food for her extended family. A 'capital hand' at making large seine nets for catching shad and herring, the striking image of her wading waist-deep in the water for hours during their annual spring runs to spawn in the upper reaches of the Tuckahoe never strayed far from Frederick's mind.

Frederick's time in Betsey's care came to an end in the late summer of 1824. He was six years old and ready to begin work as a domestic servant. Betsey did not tell him this as they set off on the long, hot 12-mile trek to Aaron Anthony's cottage on the grounds of Wye House. They walked west, towards the bay, winding their way down dusty roads, across great fields and through heavy woods, the now fifty-year-old Betsey carrying Frederick on her shoulders for long stretches. They arrived in the sweltering heat of mid-afternoon, and after gulping down some much-needed water, Frederick was sent out to play with his older brother and sisters, Perry, Sarah and Eliza, siblings he hardly knew, siblings who had made the same journey some years before him. Betsey slipped away without saying goodbye, thinking it easiest for the child. 'Fed, Fed! grandmammy gone! grandmammy gone!' called one of the children after a while. Frederick ran into the kitchen, saw it was true, and fell immediately to his knees in despair.

That night, the slave boy who in later years would advise Abraham Lincoln in the White House cried himself to sleep on a cold, stone floor.

'The Bloody Transaction'
Wye House was the vast, luxurious home of Colonel Edward Lloyd V, the tall and handsome scion of one of the oldest and wealthiest families in the state of Maryland. It was the centre of a 10,000-acre kingdom, almost a small city in itself, with beautiful gardens, a magnificent orangery full of fruits, blacksmiths,

carpenters, shoemakers, wheelwrights and even its own dock. There was also a large windmill where grist was ground, wheat having replaced tobacco as the crop on which the Lloyd fortune was based. Colonel Lloyd was one of the most important public figures of the time, a former congressman, senator and state governor. He was also well known as one of the country's most lavish entertainers, ferrying guests from the state capital, Annapolis, to Wye House on board his private sloop the *Sally Lloyd*.

The newly arrived young slave was able to sneak a tempting peek at the magnificent array of food awaiting dinner guests as he ran errands or swept out the yard. The 'glittering table' of the main house, he recalled, groaned under the profusion of beef, veal, mutton, partridges, quails, pheasants and 'teeming riches of the Chesapeake Bay'. A large garden provided 'tender asparagus', 'succulent celery', 'delicate cauliflower' and other vegetables he had never seen before. The dairy, too, poured forth 'its rich donations of fragrant cheese, golden butter and delicious cream to heighten the attraction of the gorgeous, unending round of feasting'. There were also figs, raisins, almonds and juicy grapes from Spain, wines and brandies from France, teas from China and coffee from Java.

On his death in 1834, a local paper, the *Baltimore Republican*, described how Lloyd was 'as remarkable for the munificence of his private hospitality as for his public spirit'. The paper failed to mention that it was a 'munificence' built on the back of slave labour. Slaves had worked the Lloyd land for more than a century, the family acquiring a reputation as one of the harshest masters in Maryland. The Colonel Lloyd whom Frederick knew owned more than 500 slaves. They were poorly clothed, poorly fed and kept out of sight of the main house. 'The sleeping apartments — if they may be called such — have little regard to comfort or decency,' Frederick wrote of the sheds in which the slaves lived. 'Old and young, male and female, married and single, drop down upon the common clay floor, each covering up with his or her blanket — the only protection they have from cold or exposure.'

Frederick was at something of a remove from the majority of slaves at Wye House, living in the Anthony cottage instead of the desperate slave quarters. He was, however, just as cold and hungry as the other slaves, scrabbling for food and sleeping on the floor of a small closet in the kitchen. He was quite lonely too, for although surrounded by relatives, he never forged a bond to match that which he had shared with his grandmother. The love and tenderness that had alleviated earlier hardships had disappeared.

It was not long before Frederick got his first real taste of slavery, waking up one morning to the sight of Aaron Anthony pulling the clothes off his fifteen-year-old Aunt Hester's back. Having earlier refused her owner's predatory advances, she had been caught out at night with one of the Lloyd slaves, a boy her own age named Ned Roberts. An enraged Anthony tied her hands to a hook in the kitchen ceiling, rolled up his sleeves and whipped her naked back until blood dripped down to the floor. 'No words, no tears, no prayers from his gory victim seemed to move his iron heart from its bloody purpose. The louder she screamed, the harder he whipped; and where the blood ran fastest, there he whipped longest. He would whip her to make her scream, and whip her to make her hush; and not until overcome by fatigue would he cease to swing the blood-clotted cowskin.' Young Frederick turned away in horror, hiding until 'the bloody transaction' was over. It was the first such scene he had ever witnessed; it would not be the last: his memoirs are replete with the beatings of slaves by the cruel and callous overseers at Wye House.

A more positive experience at Wye House was the friendship Frederick forged with Aaron Anthony's married daughter, Lucretia Auld, who was about twenty years old. 'Miss Lucretia', as Frederick always called her, lived in the simple stone cottage with her father and new husband, Thomas Auld, the captain of the *Sally Lloyd*. Her two elder brothers, Andrew and Richard, also stayed occasionally. 'In a family where there was so much that was harsh, cold and indifferent, the slightest word or look of kindness passed, with me, for its full value,' Frederick wrote. 'Miss Lucretia . . . bestowed upon me such words and looks.' Just as important were the pieces of bread she sometimes sneaked to him when no one was looking. She also washed the blood from his face when he got into a fight with another boy, wetting a 'nice piece of white linen' with her own balsam. For Frederick, these acts were 'sunbeams of humane treatment', finding their way into his soul through the 'iron grating of my house of bondage'.

We can never know what sign of precocity, what quirk, the young lady saw in Frederick. He was certainly a bright boy, by all accounts a clever mimic and good singer. Perhaps she was just starved of company, with the great house out of bounds, a father who was cold, stern and uncommunicative, a husband often away on Colonel Lloyd's business, and brothers — Andrew especially — who were heavy drinkers. She may also have heard the whispers concerning Frederick's birth — that he was her half-brother. Whatever the cause, it was a connection that would soon shape Frederick's life indelibly.

In 1826 the ageing and increasingly unhealthy Aaron Anthony was moved on from his position at Wye House. He took his family and slaves to one of his Tuckahoe farms. Frederick, eight years old, was ready to be put to work in the fields, the most typical of all slave experiences. This would have been his fate but for the extraordinary, generous and genuinely altruistic intervention of Lucretia Auld, who arranged for him to be sent to Baltimore, the great shipbuilding city across the Chesapeake Bay, where Thomas's brother, Hugh Auld, and his wife, Sophia, wanted a black boy to serve as a companion to their young son, as was common practice at the time. Frederick was delighted, describing the time before his departure as one of the 'happiest' of his childhood. He spent the best part of three days washing the 'plantation scurf' off his body, 'Miss Lucretia' having promised him a pair of trousers if he got clean. This 'was almost a sufficient motive, not only to induce me to scrub off the *mange* (as pig drovers would call it), but the skin as well'.

Frederick, clearly, did not feel much sense of loss at the prospect of leaving his family and the Eastern Shore.

'This Mystery of Reading'

'Instead of the cold, damp floor of my old master's kitchen, I found myself on carpets; for the corn bag in winter, I now had a good straw bed, well furnished with covers; for the coarse cornmeal in the morning, I now had good bread, and mush occasionally; for my poor tow-linen shirt, reaching to my knees, I had good clean clothes.' Frederick's world had changed — and for the better. He was still a slave, the property of Aaron Anthony, but not treated as one. His new master, Hugh Auld, a carpenter trying to set up his own shipbuilding business, was too busy to pay much heed to the new arrival. Frederick's new mistress, however, 'Miss Sopha', was exceptionally kind, welcoming him into the house with a warm smile. Coming from a simple country family that had never owned slaves, she treated Frederick as well as her own son, and he soon came to regard her as 'something more akin to a mother, than a

12

slaveholding mistress'. He also grew close to the little boy, Tommy.

Frederick's new home in the busy ship-building district of Fells Point was a world away from Wye House, and he was at first disorientated by the sheer scale and noise of the place, wagons and carriages clattering loudly through the narrow cobblestone streets at all hours. He started to run errands, however, such as fetching pails of water from the town pump, and soon learned his way around the maze of streets that all seemed to end in busy dockyards, noting with amazement how everyone, even the black men and women he saw, seemed to wear shoes.

Back at home, Sophia, a pious Methodist, often read the Bible aloud, awakening Frederick's curious mind 'to this *mystery* of reading'. The young, curly-headed slave asked her to teach him, which she did, unquestioningly. They read passages from the Bible together, slowly and carefully. Frederick quickly mastered the alphabet and learned to spell words three or four letters long. The lessons were ended by Hugh Auld who, although not a slaveholder, still held the prejudices of the age. 'Learning would spoil the best nigger in the world,' he declared coldly, warning his wife off any further lessons. Nevertheless, a door had been opened in Frederick's mind, never to be closed. He read in secret from the Bible, a spare Methodist hymn book and later young Tommy's discarded school books. He also asked his young white playmates on the streets to act as teachers — skin colour no impediment to the forging of friendships at that young age. He paid his *'tuition fee'* to these boys with bread or biscuits taken from home. Later, Frederick would teach himself to write, drawing inspiration from the way shipbuilders made marks on the different pieces of timber — 'S.' for starboard, 'L.' for larboard (or port), 'L.A.' for larboard aft and so on. He would copy these marks onto the pavement with chalk, again asking his young white friends for help.

Before that, however, came a trepidatious return to the Eastern Shore.

'Cash! Cash! Cash! For Negroes'
In October 1827, Frederick was called back to the Tuckahoe Creek. Aaron Anthony had died the previous November and his property, including about thirty slaves — essentially the extended Bailey clan — was to be divided up between his two sons and Thomas Auld. Frederick was reunited — briefly — with his beloved grandmother, as the slaves were lined

up on one of Anthony's farms to be assessed and examined by two lawyers. The value reached was $2,800 (about $210,000 in today's money).

'What an assemblage!' Frederick wrote of the humiliating experience. 'Men and women, young and old, married and single; moral and intellectual beings, in open contempt of their humanity, levelled at a blow with horses, sheep, horned cattle, and swine . . . and all subjected to the same narrow inspection, to ascertain their value in gold and silver — the only standard of worth applied by slaveholders to slaves! How vividly at that moment did the brutalizing power of slavery flash before me! Personality swallowed up in the sordid idea of property! Manhood lost in chattelhood!'

Frederick's fears were heightened by the fact that his protector, Lucretia Auld, had also died by this time, in the summer of 1827, perhaps after giving birth to a daughter, Amanda. The prospect of ending up the slave of the cruel and drunken Andrew Anthony was now very real. This, Frederick makes clear, was seen as a certain prelude to being sold south to new slave states like Alabama and Mississippi. This was the ultimate terror for most slaves, to be torn away from family and friends, the only pleasures in their harsh lives, and put to work on vast plantations of cotton and rice that matched the infamous sugar islands of the Caribbean in their severity. No tears at the prospect of a final and complete separation from parent, child or spouse could halt the process. Such had been the case in Frederick's own family, with an aunt, Maryann, and three cousins sold to a firm of Alabama slave traders in 1825, never to be heard from again.

'Spurred by the South's insatiable appetite for black bodies to fuel its explosively expanding new cotton kingdom, slave buyers by the score pushed into Virginia and Maryland offering 'Cash! Cash! Cash! for Negroes,'' Dickson J. Preston has written of early nineteenth-century America. They were particularly keen on young, strong blacks and found many willing sellers, the slow but steady decline of labour-intensive tobacco farming making slaves something of a burden for many masters. Some slave owners met this new economic reality by granting their slaves freedom (particularly the older males) and leaving them to fend for themselves. These manumissions were cost-saving exercises rather than acts of humanity, but they had the important effect of increasing the number of free blacks living and working in large cities like Baltimore — America's 'Black Capital'. Other slave owners, however, were quick to take the money on offer, the

Chesapeake Bay region exporting about 124,000 enslaved workers in the decade after 1810.

As prophesied, some of the slaves given to the dissolute Andrew Anthony, including Frederick's sister Sarah, were soon sold south. Frederick, however, escaped this most fearful of fates, assigned instead to Lucretia's widower, Thomas Auld. Perhaps in respect of his deceased wife's wishes for the bright slave boy, Auld sent Frederick straight back to Baltimore, to the welcoming arms of 'Miss Sopha'. Frederick would spend the next five-and-a-half vital, formative years of life in the great port city of the Chesapeake Bay, an urban hotbed where slaves and free blacks intermingled reasonably freely, if not always happily, with new immigrants from Europe, including, of course, Irish immigrants and workers.

'New Ireland'
Irish immigrants had been arriving in Maryland since the first years of the colony. They travelled over on ships from ports like Cork or Kinsale that traded textiles and provisions for tobacco and West Indian sugar. Many were indentured servants, men and (less often) women who signed contracts (indentures) to work a

set period of time, usually about five years, in exchange for free passage and the promise of some land or money at the end of their term, their so-called 'freedom dues'. The chance of a better life in the New World, of setting up as an independent farmer or craftsman, made temporary servitude a palatable choice, place names like 'New Munster' and 'New Ireland' paying testament to the mark made by these early Irish settlers and servants. A few of these early immigrants, most notably Charles Carroll from Offaly, made great successes of themselves, acquiring wealth and prestige. The grand majority, however, toiled away as simple manual labourers or domestic servants all their lives, unheralded and unrecorded. They worked in rural Maryland at first but soon found their way to emerging cities like Baltimore.

Baltimore — the very name was Irish in origin, bestowed upon the city in honour of Cecil Calvert, the second Lord Baltimore, an English nobleman and founder of Maryland in 1634. Calvert's father, George, a high-ranking politician in the court of King James I, had been granted the title in 1625, the name deriving from some lands the family held in Ireland. Starting out as a collection of small hamlets on the banks of the Patapsco River, Baltimore grew exponentially through the second half of the eighteenth century to become the third largest city in America, after New York and Philadelphia. It owed much of its success to the ingenuity of an Irish-born physician, John Stevenson, who in 1750 sent a cargo of flour from Baltimore to Ireland as an experiment. The flour, which came from the wheat fields of Pennsylvania, was well received on account of its purity and resistance to mould. A major trade was born, Baltimore morphing from a small, sleepy harbour into an important port that traded with the world.

The heavy work on the docks proved a natural home for many Irish immigrants in Baltimore. They could also be found digging canals and building railroads, including the famous Baltimore & Ohio, the first railway built in America. They worked alongside free blacks and slaves as well as other immigrants from Europe. 'The Irish and Negroes are kept separate from each other, for fear of serious consequences,' a visitor to the Chesapeake & Ohio Canal observed in 1826. However, it would be wrong to overemphasise the degree of animosity that existed between the Irish and blacks in America at this time, Jay Dolan describing how they coexisted quite peacefully in shared neighbourhoods in cities like Philadelphia and how in the Five Points bars of New York 'men and women, black and Irish, drank, sang and danced to tunes that blended Irish and African musical styles'. In the South, too, the Irish and blacks — sharing the same low social status — often lived near each other and shared daily contact with each other. There was certainly some friction, the Irish in the South — recently arrived or otherwise — far from immune to racism and slaveholding. Nevertheless, it was only in the mid to late 1830s that racial tensions really came to the fore, the ever-increasing numbers of Irish immigrants and free blacks competing with each other for the same unskilled jobs, often deliberately pitched against each other, indeed, by rapacious white bosses.

It is no surprise, therefore, that the Irish dockers unloading the scow of stones in Baltimore in the early 1830s should have talked to the young Frederick Bailey, as he was then still known, so kindly and affably.

'The Rights of Man'
Frederick already knew something of Ireland before meeting the two dockers: the first book he ever purchased, *The Columbian Orator*, included an extract from a speech by the Irish politician and rebel Arthur O'Connor. Speaking before the Irish House of Commons in

1795, O'Connor promised to 'risk everything dear to me on earth' in the quest for Catholic emancipation, the campaign to end the Penal Laws under which the Catholic majority laboured in Ireland. 'I got a bold and powerful denunciation of oppression,' Frederick wrote of O'Connor's speech, 'and a most brilliant vindication of the rights of man.'

Bought from a book shop in Fells Point with fifty cents he surreptitiously earned shining shoes, the *Orator* was a compendium of heroic, patriotic speeches boys learned at school or for public speaking competitions. The contributions ranged from the Greek philosopher Socrates and the Roman politician Cato to the soldier-statesmen George Washington and Napoleon Bonaparte. It was immensely popular, one of a handful of essential texts found in American homes, alongside the Bible, a spelling book and a farmer's almanac. Frederick, who enjoyed a remarkable degree of freedom for a slave under the generally lax watch of the Aulds, read it for hours at a time, just like the young Abraham Lincoln, checking the many words he did not know with a dictionary, making notes in the margins, re-reading passages again and again until he grasped their full meaning. Frederick's vocabulary grew immeasurably. He also gained important lessons for the future in the art of public speaking from the wide-ranging introduction, which emphasised the importance of pronunciation and the effective use of gestures. Most importantly, however, the constant invocation of words like liberty, freedom and equality made a deep impression on his rapidly developing young mind.

Frederick was also learning more and more, albeit often obliquely, about slavery. He read of attempts to close down slave markets in the nearby Washington, D.C. and may have heard fragments of talk about Nat Turner's bloodily suppressed slave rebellion in neighbouring Virginia. He certainly heard the clank of chains as slaves were led out at night from their slave pens in the city to the harbour prior to sailing south. Words like 'abolition' also began to filter into his consciousness, through overheard conversations or newspaper articles. 'Of *who* or *what* these [abolitionists] were, I was totally ignorant. I found, however, that whatever they might be, they were . . . hated and . . . abused by slaveholders . . . If a slave, for instance, had made good his escape from slavery, it was generally alleged, that he had been persuaded and assisted by the abolitionists.'

Frederick's trusty second-hand copy of *The Columbian Orator*, hidden from Hugh

Auld's view in the loft of his house, also had a memorable piece on slavery — an imagined dialogue between a master and his slave — that young Frederick memorised. This short section, Dickson J. Preston has observed, carefully slipped in among the worthy, patriotic speeches by Caleb Bingham, the anti-slavery Massachusetts educator who compiled the *Orator*, would have shocked racist Baltimoreans if they had ever bothered to read it.

The 'Dialogue' begins with the master recapturing his slave, who has twice tried to run away. The master has treated the slave well, and does not understand why he wants to escape. It continues, in part:

Master: It is in the order of Providence that one man should become subservient to another. It ever has been so, and ever will be. I found the custom, and did not make it.

Slave: You cannot but be sensible, that the robber who puts a pistol to your breast may make just the same plea. Providence gives him a power over your life and property; it gave my enemies a power over my liberty.

Master: Gratitude! I repeat, gratitude! Have I not endeavoured ever since I possessed you to alleviate your misfortunes by kind treatment? Consider how much worse your condition might have been under another master.

Slave: You have done nothing for me more than for your working cattle. Are they not well fed and tended?

Master: But it was my intention not only to make your life tolerably comfortable at present, but to provide for you in your old age.

Slave: Alas! Is a life like mine, torn from country, friends and all I held dear, and compelled to toil under the burning sun for a master, worth thinking about for old age? No; the sooner it ends, the sooner I shall obtain that relief for which my soul pants.

The debate continues, and by the end the slave has convinced his master of the immorality of slavery. In doing so, he wins his freedom.
   'It is scarcely necessary to say, that a dialogue, with such an origin, and such an ending — read when the fact of my being a

slave was a constant burden of grief — powerfully affected me,' Frederick wrote, 'and I could not help feeling that the day might come when the well-directed answers made by the slave to the master, in this instance, would find their counterpart in myself.'

The teenage Frederick began to read this and other passages aloud to the boys — black and white — with whom he played and worked on the docks, the powerfully built and increasingly strong-willed youth already stepping into the role of orator and leader. The thought of being a slave for life weighed ever more heavily on his heart, and dreams of escape began to enter his mind. Then, suddenly, in the spring of 1833, Frederick's Baltimore world was torn apart: an argument between the brothers sent him back across the water to the town of St Michaels, where his newly remarried owner Thomas Auld now ran a store and post office.

Frederick, like every slave, was still not in control of his own destiny.

'The Dark Night of Slavery'

Frederick was fifteen years old when he landed on the wharf of St Michaels, a run-down town far removed from the bustle of Baltimore. Life with Thomas Auld and his new wife, Rowena, was fractious from the beginning, any lingering regard for the now 38-year-old Auld, a man who had twice facilitated his path out of the Eastern Shore, dispelled when Frederick saw him whip his disabled cousin Henny. Rowena, meanwhile, who unlike her husband came from an old slaveholding family, despised all the 'worthless niggers' in the house — Frederick, his sister Eliza, their Aunt Priscilla and cousin Henny. She treated them coldly and let them go hungry. They, in turn, were constantly 'forgetting' to carry out chores, one of the age-old means of slave resistance. Frederick, who chafed under the new restrictions after years of relative freedom in Baltimore, also got involved in a short-lived Sunday school for blacks, earning the reputation of a 'bad nigger' around the bigoted town.

Within a year, the increasingly rebellious Frederick, who Auld felt had been ruined by the city, was sent to work as a field-hand for Edward Covey, a few miles outside St Michaels. Covey was a poor but hardworking tenant farmer in his late twenties. He was also extremely ambitious and cruel, with a reputation as a 'Negro breaker' among blacks in the area. He whipped Frederick — who had little understanding of farm animals or implements — almost as soon as he arrived.

26

This was the first real whipping of Frederick's life. Covey would go on to whip him every week for six months, cutting his back severely and leaving large welts on his flesh. The hard work and constant beatings wore the slave down. 'I was broken in body, soul and spirit. My natural elasticity was crushed, my intellect languished, the disposition to read departed, the cheerful spark that lingered about my eye died; the dark night of slavery closed in upon me; and behold a man transformed into a brute.'

In early August 1834, Frederick collapsed from sunstroke while threshing wheat. He dragged himself to some shade but was kicked in the side and beaten over the head by Covey. Bloodied and bruised, barefoot and faint, he ran 7 miles through fields and woods to St Michaels. Frederick begged to be sent to work on another farm. Thomas Auld, however, seemingly unmoved by the wretched, blood-covered figure trembling before him, insisted that he return to Covey. Frederick obeyed, but resolved to defend himself next time.

Covey was on the attack again within days, but Frederick fought back. 'I found my strong fingers firmly attached to the throat of my cowardly tormentor . . . I flung him on the ground several times, when he meant to have hurled me there. I held him so firmly by the throat, that his blood followed my nails.' They wrestled and grappled with each other for a long time, to the point of exhaustion. 'He held me, and I held him.' Frederick could have been whipped or even hanged for his resistance. Instead, the fight proved a turning point in his life. 'It rekindled in my breast the smouldering embers of liberty; it brought up my Baltimore dreams, and revived a sense of my own manhood. I was a changed being after that fight. I was *nothing* before; I WAS A MAN NOW.'

Frederick stayed at Covey's farm until the end of the year, but was not struck or whipped again. The only explanation he could come up with — one he admitted was not entirely satisfactory — was that Covey, the famed 'Negro breaker', was ashamed to have it known that he had been 'mastered by a boy of sixteen'. There may, however, have been another force at work, Dickson J. Preston suggesting that Thomas Auld, despite his cold rebuff that desperate night in St Michaels, interjected on his slave's behalf, ordering Covey to ease off.

'Band of Brothers'
Frederick was hired out to William Freeland, an older farmer on the Eastern Shore, in

January 1835. The land was worn out from years of tobacco planting and needed hard work to produce paying crops of wheat and corn. Nevertheless, it was a much fairer environment, with warm clothes, good sleeping quarters and no beatings. Frederick stayed with Freeland — 'the best master I ever had, until I became my own master' — for more than a year. He began to take some pride in his work, even if it was just spreading manure over the fields, and forged perhaps the deepest friendships of his life, with John and Henry Harris, brothers owned by Freeland, and some other slaves in the area. 'I never loved, esteemed, or confided in men, more than I did in these. They were as true as steel, and no band of brothers could have been more loving.'

Frederick worked hard, played games and drank with these young men. But he also helped a number of them learn to read and write, his literacy giving him a special status among the slaves. At one point he had more than twenty students at the secret Sunday school held under an oak tree in the summer, his much-thumbed copy of *The Columbian Orator* being put to good use again. Dreams of freedom, too, returned to Frederick's mind, as he looked out across the broad waters of the bay and watched steamers head north to the newly built Chesapeake and Delaware Canal and through to Philadelphia, in the free state of Pennsylvania. On New Year's Day 1836, he resolved to put these dreams into action.

Escape by land from the long peninsula deemed next to impossible, Frederick started to disclose to his friends a bold plan to steal a log canoe from a neighbouring farm, paddle furiously to the head of the bay — a distance of some 70 miles — and slip into Pennsylvania. The time chosen was early April, just before Easter, when restrictions on slaves were usually relaxed. There would be rough waters to contend with and 'slave-catchers' prowling the border areas to avoid. What awaited them in the North was also somewhat vague. Frederick, for instance, knew of New York City, Pennsylvania, Delaware and New Jersey but not New York State or Massachusetts. Nevertheless, the band of brothers continued to prepare, anxious and excited at the prospect before them. Their plan, however, was discovered — Frederick never found out how — and the five would-be escapees were rounded up as they started work on the day that was to have been their last in slavery.

Tied together behind two horses, Frederick and his friends were marched barefooted the 15 miles from Freeland's farm to the county jail in Easton. It was extremely hot and dusty and they were jeered all along the way by small crowds. Before leaving the farm, Freeland's elderly mother gave some biscuits to the Harris brothers, boys she had known all their lives. She then turned to Frederick. 'You devil! You yellow devil!' she shouted at the strident-looking young man already marked out as the ringleader. 'It was you that put it into the heads of Henry and John to run away. But for *you*, you *long-legged yellow devil*, Henry and John would never have thought of running away.'

'The ever dreaded slave life in Georgia, Louisiana and Alabama — from which escape is next to impossible — now . . . stared me in the face,' Frederick wrote, the jail in Easton soon swarming with excited slave traders. But there was no trial, no hanging, no being sold south. The young men stuck together, denied everything. No escape attempt had actually been made; nothing could be proved. Within a few days, the four other slaves were taken home by their masters, William Freeland and William Hambleton. They went back to work unharmed. Thomas Auld, however, under pressure from his father-in-law and with slave traders knocking on his door, left the eighteen-year-old Frederick to languish in his cell a little longer. Everyone knew he was the ringleader — despite being the youngest, bar one, of the group — and custom dictated that he should be punished as a warning to other slaves. Auld had beaten Frederick's cousin Henny and perhaps even Frederick once. He had also hired him out to the brutish Covey. Nevertheless, Auld, far from the stingy, feeble villain of Frederick's later writings, struggled with the idea of sending him south. Their lives had been too long intertwined, the curly-headed little boy singing songs for Auld's first wife, Lucretia, at the cottage. Perhaps promises had been made to look after her favourite? There have also been suggestions that it was Auld, not old Aaron Anthony, who was Frederick's father, the then captain of the *Sally Lloyd* happening upon the attractive Harriet Bailey on an errand to Wye House.

And so, the far-from-affluent Auld turned his back on the $1,000 a slave of Frederick's age and strength was sure to fetch (about $75,000 in today's money). He talked loudly of selling him to 'a friend in Alabama', but this was only for public consumption. Instead, he sent Frederick back to Baltimore to live with his brother Hugh again and learn a trade. There was even the vague promise of emancipation when he reached the age of twenty-five.

In truth, he was setting him free.

'A Free Man'

Back in Baltimore, Frederick was sent to work as an apprentice caulker in William Gardiner's shipyard. Frederick, however, learned little of caulking, the back-breaking means of making wooden boats watertight, by driving fibrous material into the wedge-shaped seams between boards. Instead, he was treated as general factotum about the yard, called a dozen ways every minute of the day. 'Fred, come carry this timber yonder . . . Fred, go get a fresh can of water . . . Fred, go quick and get the crowbar . . . Halloo, nigger! Come turn this grindstone . . . I say, darkey, blast your eyes, why don't you heat up some pitch?'

When Frederick had been a young teenager helping out around the docks, racism had not really been evident, the black and white ship carpenters often working side by side. This had changed by the time he returned from the Eastern Shore, the ever-increasing numbers of white immigrants, free blacks and hired-out slaves in Baltimore competing desperately with each other for the same jobs. Even the white boys he had played with had grown up and absorbed the prevailing anti-black prejudice of the times. In later years, Frederick would write philosophically about how the 'white slave' and the 'black slave' were both robbed by the same system. There was, however, no time to be thoughtful as he was bullied and pushed about by the carpenters and white apprentices at Gardiner's yard. One day, after about eight months in the job, he was attacked by four white apprentices, including the very Irish-sounding Ned Hayes. Frederick fought back, as always, but the blows across the head and body with bricks, handspikes and fists burst his eyeball and left his face scarred and bloody. The assault had taken place in full view of fifty or so of the carpenters employed at the yard, who instead of trying to stop it had called out 'Kill him — kill him — kill the damned nigger'.

Things improved for Frederick after this brush with death — he never saw it as anything less. He went to work at Asa Price's yard where Hugh Auld was foreman (Auld's own shipbuilding business had closed down). Frederick learned the caulking trade and within a year was earning the comparatively substantial sum of $9 a week during busy periods, all of which, of course, was collected by Auld. By the summer of 1838, however, Frederick was allowed to hire himself out. This was increasingly common in Baltimore. For slaves, it meant a degree of autonomy over their lives; for masters, a guaranteed fee and less expense incurred in board and lodging. In Frederick's case, he would be allowed to find his own work and collect his own wages provided he paid Auld $3 a week — irrespective of whether or not he had worked — and supplied his own bed, board and tools.

The twenty-year-old Frederick embraced this new degree of relative freedom. He found lodgings in Fells Point and, although a slave, got involved in Baltimore's vibrant, expanding free black world. He joined clubs, forged friendships with other articulate young blacks and even got engaged to a free black woman, Anna Murray, a domestic servant five years his senior. He also started to learn about the Underground Railroad, the surreptitious network of safe houses for fugitives along well-established routes, even helping some runaway slaves plan their escapes.

When an argument with Hugh Auld brought an end to Frederick's partial freedom, the never-distant thoughts of escape rushed back to the fore. And so it was that after several weeks of careful planning he boarded a train of the Baltimore & Ohio Railroad (B&O) on 3 September 1838, jumping on just as it set off. This new line of the B&O went north from Baltimore to Wilmington, in the slave state of Delaware.

From there, steamboat and rail connections brought passengers to Philadelphia and on to New York. There were many obstacles to cross, the B&O extremely conscious of runaway slaves trying to use their trains. Determined to protect masters' property, black people were allowed to travel only by day, and always in possession of their 'free papers', a passport-like document that detailed their appearance and certified their free status.

Frederick obtained a sailor's protection pass (an equivalent to free papers) from a friend. It had the image of an American eagle on the front. He also bought some sailor's clothes — a red shirt, black cravat and tarpaulin hat — with some of Anna's savings. Frederick did not really look like the man described in the papers. Nevertheless, his years on the docks helped him play the part of a seaman. 'I knew a ship from stem to stern, and from keelson to cross-trees, and could talk sailor like an 'old salt'.'

The train was halfway to Delaware before the conductor entered the dusty, dirty carriage reserved for blacks.

'You have something to show that you are a free man, have you not?' the conductor asked.

'Yes sir,' Frederick answered. 'I have a paper with the American eagle on it that will carry me around the world.'

Assuaged by Frederick's nonchalant response or simply eager to get to the end of the crowded black carriage, the conductor glanced at the pass, took the fare and moved on. There were several more dangerous moments, but Frederick survived them all, arriving in New York City early the next morning. He was, at last, 'a *free man*'.

Frederick made his way to the home of David Ruggles, a black journalist who headed the New York Underground Railroad. Anna joined him a few days later. They were married on 15 September, Frederick having carried a new wedding suit alongside his *Columbian Orator* and a few other possessions in his sailor's satchel. With slave-catchers scouring the streets, New York City was no place for runaways. Frederick and Anna moved on quickly, boarding a coach to the safer environment of New Bedford, Massachusetts, a prosperous whaling town with grand houses overlooking the harbour, the setting for the opening scenes of *Moby-Dick*. They spent their first few weeks living with Nathan Johnson, a black Quaker, and his family. Frederick Bailey, the fugitive slave, needed a new name. Johnson had just finished reading Walter Scott's *The Lady of the Lake* and was so impressed with the bravery of one of the protagonists, James Douglas, that he recommended it to Frederick. An extra 's' was added by mistake.

Frederick Douglass was born.

2

Abolitionists

The fevered edge to Frederick Douglass's last months in Baltimore faded away as he settled into life in New Bedford, a town with a well-established black population. He rented a small apartment, worked as a caulker and labourer and joined a local black church. He and Anna started a family. They also played the violin together — Anna teaching Frederick — and enjoyed dinners with new friends. The Douglasses were quite poor their first winter and there were still some racist jibes to put up with on the docks. Nevertheless, a relatively safe, comfortable existence was within reach.

Douglass, however, could not switch off his slave past so easily; his dreams were plagued by the 'dead, heavy footsteps' and 'piteous cries' of the chained gangs of slaves he had heard marching to the docks in Baltimore at night prior to sailing south. He began to speak at local anti-slavery groups, his words picked up by *The Liberator*, the radical abolitionist newspaper edited by William

Lloyd Garrison. It was not long before Douglass saw the tall, gaunt, passionate and improbably charismatic figure of Garrison speak in person. A few years later, Douglass was thrust even deeper into the Garrisonian world, delivering his first major public speech to a meeting of the Massachusetts Anti-Slavery Society in Nantucket in late August 1841.

'My speech on this occasion is about the only one I ever made, of which I do not remember a single connected sentence,' Douglass recalled. He was twenty-three years old, a fugitive slave, addressing a room full of anti-slavery luminaries. His hands shook as he spoke and his legs felt like they were about to give way. Douglass worked through the initial nervousness to deliver an emotional speech that had the predominantly white audience straining forward to make out the features of the tall, attractive and remarkably articulate young man. 'Have we been listening to a thing, a piece of property or to a man?' Garrison demanded of the audience. 'A man! A man!' came the united response.

Douglass was approached that very evening to become a paid agent of the Massachusetts Anti-Slavery Society. He would go on the road and tell of his experience of slavery.

'The Traffic of Men-Body'
The first slave ship to America landed near Jamestown, Virginia, in late August 1619. It was a Dutch-flagged corsair or pirate ship named the *White Lyon*, its cargo of '20 and odd Negroes' quickly traded for food with the governor of the recently established English colony.

Captured during fighting in the Portuguese colony of Angola on the west coast of Africa, the story of the *White Lyon* slaves is emblematic of the horrors inflicted upon the millions of Africans forcibly transported across the Atlantic. They had originally been part of a larger group of 350 slaves loaded in leg irons and neck chains onto a Portuguese slaver, the *San Juan Bautista*, in the Angolan capital, Luanda. Their destination had been Veracruz in Mexico, the trade in African slaves to the European, primarily Spanish and Portuguese, colonies of the Caribbean and Central and South America having taken root more than a century before, not long after Christopher Columbus's epochal voyage. These first African slaves were used to complement the newly conquered indigenous workforces. They worked, for example, in the gold mines of Hispaniola and the sugar fields of Cuba and Brazil. However, it was not long before war, European diseases and overwork

41

eviscerated the native populations. Demand for the more robust African slaves grew exponentially, turning the transatlantic slave trade into a devastatingly major enterprise.

Crossing the Atlantic, many of the slaves crammed into the dark and dirty hold of the *San Juan Bautista* died of disease. Then, nearing Veracruz, the ship was attacked by the *White Lyon* and another corsair, the *Treasurer*. The pirate ships opened fire on the poorly defended slaver, forcing it to heave to and allow their captains on board. A large number of the slaves were dragged from one ship to another, mid-ocean. The two corsairs then made their way up the Florida Strait to Virginia. The *White Lyon* was the first to reach land, depositing its traumatised cargo on a strange and frightening new shore.

The trade in slaves, although slow at first, gradually insinuated itself into the fabric of American — especially Southern — society. African slaves were a vital source of cheap labour for the white settlers, especially when the numbers of indentured white labourers from Europe fell away in the last third of the seventeenth century. Initially, as David Reynolds has observed, the distinction between slavery and servitude was somewhat 'fuzzy'. The racial divide hardened, however, as the number of slaves started to soar. The

42

white settlers felt threatened and put in place laws — the notorious slave codes — that made clear the subservient status of black slaves. Slave owners were also given virtually a free hand in how they disciplined slaves. Whipping was routine, but slaves could also be mutilated or even burned to death quite legally.

By the time of the American Revolution there were about half a million slaves in the thirteen colonies soon to form the United States. This was out of a total population of just under 2.5 million. In every colony from Maryland southwards, at least one third of the population was enslaved, significantly more in South Carolina and Georgia. These slaves, second-class citizens in the eyes of the law and subhuman in the eyes of many masters, worked as domestic servants, carpenters, blacksmiths and butchers in northern cities like New York, cleared forests and picked tobacco in Virginia and Maryland, cultivated rice in the vast plantations of the Deep South. The slave system seemed strong — despite periodic slave revolts — an immutable feature of the American landscape. And yet there were fractures in the edifice, with Thomas Jefferson, a slave owner himself, denouncing the slave trade in his first draft of the Declaration of Independence. It was an 'execrable commerce', the future president wrote, one that violated the 'most sacred rights of life and liberty in the persons of a distant people [i.e. Africans] . . . captivating and carrying them into slavery in another hemisphere'. This strong statement did not make it into the final draft of the Declaration, removed for the sake of unity between the states. However, the fact that it was written at all was a sign that dissenting voices had finally started to push anti-slavery onto the political agenda.

As early as 1646 Puritan magistrates in Massachusetts had condemned the 'haynos and crying sinn of man stealing', ordering the return of two captured Africans to their native land. In February 1688, four German-born Quakers from Pennsylvania, the model Quaker colony founded by William Penn, drafted a set of resolutions against slavery, or what they called 'the traffic of men-body'. They had been shocked at the inconsistency of Quakers, refugees from Europe's religious intolerance, buying and selling people against their will. Quakers, however, would go on to play a disproportionately large role in the anti-slavery movement, the London Yearly Meeting, to which many American Quakers still looked for guidance, issuing a series of anti-slavery epistles throughout the 1700s. It was also Quaker campaigners like Anthony

Benezet who brought anti-slavery to the fore of public debate in America in the 1760s and 1770s. Indeed, after many years of equivocation, the Pennsylvania Yearly Meeting of 1776 finally banned Quakers in America from owning slaves. Benezet had already made contact with British anti-slavery activists by this time, Britain having taken over from Spain, Portugal and the Netherlands as the dominant force in slave trade. Parliament was petitioned, politicians lobbied, books and pamphlets published in profusion. Anti-slavery was becoming a transatlantic crusade. The outbreak of the American Revolution, however, 'dramatically subordinated the question of slavery to other priorities'.

The immediate aftermath of the American Revolution saw several states in the North, such as Vermont, New Hampshire and Pennsylvania, move to ban or partially abolish slavery. Others like New York and New Jersey followed more reluctantly. The Revolution, however, was far from a watershed moment for slaves. Action in the North, which accounted for just 6 per cent of the enslaved population, was one matter, but what of the South? For every state making a move against slavery, there seemed to be another slave state waiting to join the Union, like Kentucky in 1792 and Tennessee in 1796. The Louisiana

Purchase of 1803 — where a vast area of land stretching from the Mississippi River to the Rocky Mountains was bought from France — also brought thousands more slaves under American jurisdiction. The cotton boom, too, gave a fresh impetus to slavery. Even the passage of legislation prohibiting the slave trade in 1807 — the same year that a similar law was passed in Britain — was not a cause of celebration. Slaves could still be imported, albeit illegally, through Spanish Florida quite easily. Furthermore, unlike the sugar islands of the Caribbean, where slaves were worked so hard and died in such numbers they needed constant replenishing from Africa, American slave owners were actually more reliant on natural increase among the slave population than on the slave trade. There was also the not inconsiderable fact that while in Britain the abolition of the slave trade was seen as the triumphant end to a long moral crusade, in America a lot of support for the act came from a belief that the country already had enough people of colour. Racism rather morality got the law passed.

'I Will Be Heard'

At the time Frederick Douglass was born, America was increasingly delimited into zones of free and slave states, the Ohio River providing a rough boundary between the two. There were 1.5 million slaves (about 20 per cent of the total population) in the still-expanding United States, and although the question of slavery had been the source of discord and weak compromise among politicians, as an institution it seemed secure. The anti-slavery campaign was also in the midst of a long period of general abeyance, despite the efforts of a new generation of Quaker campaigners like Benjamin Lundy. This all changed with the arrival of the remarkable William Lloyd Garrison onto the anti-slavery scene in the late 1820s.

Born in Massachusetts in late December 1805 to a deeply religious Baptist mother and a sailor father who walked out on the family, Garrison had been a campaigning journalist and editor from his early twenties. He wanted 'to raise the moral tone of the country' and at first put his energies into the burgeoning temperance movement. Then, in 1829, he started work on the Baltimore-based *Genius of Universal Emancipation*, edited by the Quaker Lundy. (This was about the same time that the young Douglass was playing on the docks in Baltimore.) Inspired by Lundy, a thin, wispy man who had travelled on foot across much of America, quietly convincing

47

many slaveholders to manumit their slaves, Garrison took the fateful decision to make anti-slavery his life's work. More specifically, he made abolition his cause: the immediate — not gradual — emancipation of all slaves, without compensation for slave owners and without deportation of the freed people to Haiti or Africa, as proposed by other anti-slavery activists.

Garrison quickly made a name for himself, printing graphic accounts of the murders of slaves and attacking other Baltimore papers for accepting advertisements for local slave auctions. He was convicted of libel for an article denouncing a wealthy merchant's participation in the slave trade. Garrison refused to pay the fine of $50 (about three months' pay) and was jailed for forty-nine days. 'A few white victims must be sacrificed to open the eyes of this nation, and to show the tyranny of our laws,' he declared, happily assuming the mantle of a martyr. 'I am willing to be persecuted, imprisoned and bound for advocating African rights, and I should deserve to be a slave myself, if I shrunk from that duty or danger.'

Still in his mid-twenties, Garrison moved to Boston, launching *The Liberator* on 1 January 1831. 'I am aware that many object to the severity of my language, but is there not cause for severity?' he asked in the paper's first editorial, continuing:

I *will be* as harsh as truth and as uncompromising as justice. On this subject, I do not wish to think or speak or write with moderation. No! No! Tell a man whose house is on fire to give a moderate alarm; tell him to moderately rescue his wife from the hands of the ravisher; tell the mother to gradually extricate her babe from the fire into which it has fallen — but urge me not to use moderation in a cause like the present. I am in earnest — I will not equivocate — I will not excuse — I will not retreat a single inch — AND I WILL BE HEARD.

A few years later, Garrison, a lifelong advocate of non-violent moral force, was one of the main figures behind the formation of the American Anti-Slavery Society. Where previously many Americans had looked upon slavery as a distasteful relic from colonial times, a problem for future generations to resolve, increasing numbers now got involved in the cause, establishing a network of anti-slavery associations across the North. By 1838 the organisation boasted a membership of about 250,000. 'With a Biblical prophet's power and a propagandist's skill', Garrison (in the words of his biographer, Henry Mayer) had 'forced the nation to confront the most crucial moral issue in its history'. He also travelled to Britain, where the anti-slavery movement was on a high after the abolition of slavery in the British West Indies in 1833, a move that freed more than 800,000 slaves, albeit at a cost of more than £20 million in compensation for slave owners. Many African Americans, including Douglass, would celebrate 1 August (the West Indies' Emancipation Day) with much more fervour than 4 July — America's own fabled Independence Day.

Garrison was a deeply moral, deeply radical man; too radical, in the end, for many adherents. He turned away from traditional modes of political engagement, such as voting, accusing not just the two main parties (Whigs and Democrats) but the whole system of government itself of corruption. He also supported equal rights for women and attacked the established Churches for colluding with slavery. Garrison would go on to deride the Constitution, with its pledge to assist in the recapture of runaway slaves, as a 'covenant with death and an agreement with hell'. His radicalism split the movement in

1840, leading to the formation of both the Liberty Party, which believed in putting candidates forward for elections, and the American and Foreign Anti-Slavery Society, a much more moderate organisation whose members saw slavery as a grotesque anomaly in an otherwise wholesome American society.

Shorn of more than half of its members and most of its funds, the American Anti-Slavery Society was in need of a charismatic orator to champion its cause just as Douglass made his debut at Nantucket.

'Cut Out For a Hero'

'Young, ardent and hopeful, I entered upon this new life in the full gush of unsuspecting enthusiasm,' Douglass wrote. He moved his burgeoning family — a daughter Rosetta born in June 1839 and a son Lewis Henry in October 1840 — nearer to Boston, then the centre of the anti-slavery world. He was soon criss-crossing the northern states, making up to 100 speeches a year. The venues ranged from street corners, parks, town halls and chapels to Boston's famous Faneuil Hall; the audiences anywhere from single figures to several hundred. He appeared in Rochester, New York, Grafton, Massachusetts, Buffalo, New Jersey, Concord, New Hampshire and scores more towns and cities. 'I was a 'graduate from the peculiar institution,' Mr [John A.] Collins [secretary of the Massachusetts Anti-Slavery Society] used to say, when introducing me, *'with my diploma written on my back!'*"

An imposing figure and increasingly impressive speaker, Douglass quickly became the biggest draw on the anti-slavery circuit. Up to this point, the majority of anti-slavery lecturers had been whites or free blacks. The fact that Douglass was a fugitive slave, a 'chattel', a 'thing', with the mark of the whip still fresh on his back, set him on a different plane. 'The fugitive Douglass was up when we entered,' wrote Nathaniel Rogers of the *Herald of Freedom*. 'This is an extraordinary man. He was cut out for a hero ... As a speaker he has few equals. It is not declamation — but oratory, power of debate. He has wit, arguments, sarcasm, pathos — all that first rate men show in their master efforts. His voice is highly melodious and rich, and his enunciation quite elegant, and yet he has been but two or three years out of the house of bondage.' Even writers unfriendly to the cause were impressed. 'We have seldom heard a better speech before a popular assembly,' wrote a correspondent of the *Boston Courier*, 'far superior to the white speakers who followed.'

The lessons from *The Columbian Orator* had been well learned.

There were, however, 'shadows as well as sunbeams' in Douglass's new life as an anti-slavery speaker, with town halls and church doors often closed to black speakers. A subtler form of racism, meanwhile, was apparent in the snobbery and condescension of white abolitionist grandees in Boston. Douglass, for instance, was paid half what the white lecturers received, even though he was immeasurably more important to the cause. As William McFeely has written, Douglass and other black anti-slavery speakers were always treated as 'visiting artists in a production of which the white Bostonians never dreamed of losing the direction'.

Abolitionist meetings were also broken up by racist crowds across the North. In 1843, Douglass and two fellow anti-slavery speakers were attacked by a mob of about thirty men at an outdoor meeting in Pendleton, Indiana. Douglass, who was used to fist fights from his days at Gardiner's shipyard in Baltimore, found himself in the middle of the crowd, brandishing a stick. In doing so, he was violating not only Garrison's insistence on non-violence, but also white America's stern law that black men were not to raise weapons except against other black men. 'Kill the nigger, kill the damned nigger,' screamed the mob. The swing of a club broke Douglass's right hand. William A. White, another black activist, was hit by a stone on the head. When at last the mob dispersed, Douglass and White were taken to the home of a Quaker named Hardy and bandaged up.

The ever-present threat of scenes like those in Pendleton compelled the abolitionists to travel always in groups. Douglass's closest friend was Charles Lenox Remond, with whom he travelled widely across New England and the Midwest. Remond, a free black from Salem, Massachusetts, had been the most famous black anti-slavery speaker in the country before Douglass. He does not seem to have resented Douglass's rise to prominence, the strength of their bond seen in the name Douglass chose for his fourth child — Charles Lenox Douglass, born in 1844. Another son, Frederick junior, had been born two years earlier.

Remond was just back from an extended stay in Great Britain and Ireland when he got to know Douglass. He had travelled over to London for the first World Anti-Slavery Convention in the summer of 1840, staying on until the winter of 1841. He had spent six enjoyable months in Ireland towards the end of the trip, and it is easy to imagine him regaling Douglass with stories from Dublin, Cork, Limerick and other stops on his lecture tour. He must have mentioned Irish anti-slavery activists like Richard Davis Webb and Richard Allen, names that would soon mean a great deal to Douglass. Remond would also have spoken warmly of Daniel O'Connell, who, although best known as an Irish nationalist, was also an ardent anti-slavery campaigner. O'Connell's speech at the Convention was one of the most remarkable Remond ever heard. 'For thirteen years have I thought myself an abolitionist,' he reported to a friend, 'but I have been in a measure mistaken, until I listened to the scorching rebukes of the fearless O'Connell.'

At first, Douglass's own speeches to anti-slavery audiences had been limited to a general recapitulation of his life under slavery, albeit without such sensitive details as his real name or the names of his masters. (The chances of recapture were far less in Massachusetts than New York City but still had to be borne in mind, as evidenced by the case of George Latimer, an escaped slave captured in Boston in 1844 and placed in jail, avoiding reenslavement only when a wealthy abolitionist purchased his freedom.) Soon, however, he wanted to say more. 'I was now reading and thinking. New views of the subject were presented to my mind. It did not entirely satisfy me to *narrate* wrongs; I felt like *denouncing* them . . . I was growing, and needed room.'

Douglass attacked the everyday discrimination of the North that saw him thrown off trains for refusing to sit in black carriages. He also turned his attention to the role of the Church in supporting slavery.

'This Holy Book'

Douglass had been drawn powerfully to religion — particularly the Methodist faith so strong in the South — ever since Sophia Auld first read passages from the Bible to him. Forbidden to read by Hugh Auld, he would gather up 'scattered pages from this holy book' found on the streets of Baltimore and read them in secret looking for 'a word or two of wisdom'. As an introspective young teenager, Douglass joined the Bethal chapel of the African Methodist Episcopal Church in Fells Point, absorbing the thunderous messages of gospel-shouting black preachers. He was also incredibly close to a pious old free black man named Charles Lawson at this time, a rather mystical lay preacher who told Douglass the Lord had 'a great work' for him to do — prophetic-seeming words which the young slave took to heart.

Douglass's reverence for religion fell away once sent back to the Eastern Shore, where Thomas Auld and his wife Rowena prayed deeply every morning but still let their slaves almost starve. Edward Covey, another pious Methodist, would smile at slaves on Sunday mornings on the way to church before whipping them the next day. Methodist ministers, meanwhile, encouraged slaves to look down upon their 'hard, horny hands' and 'muscular frames' as proof that God had adapted them to physical labour, while their white masters, 'who have slender frames and long delicate fingers', were designed for thinking. Douglass would parody these slavery-supporting Southern ministers to great effect before audiences in the North, his gifts of mimicry and deep and dextrous voice coming to the fore as he spread out his arms, looked up at the ceiling and, in the manner of a minister addressing the black pews, intoned: 'And you too, my friends, have souls of infinite value — souls that will live through endless happiness or misery in eternity. Oh, labour diligently to make your calling and election sure. Oh, receive into your souls these words of the holy apostle — 'Servants, be obedient unto your masters.''

This quoting of the Bible (Ephesians 6:5)

in support of slavery would have appalled John Wesley, the founding father of Methodism in England. Deeply committed to social justice, Wesley had attacked what he called 'this execrable villainy' in his *Thoughts upon Slavery* (1774) and other writings. Arriving in America during the Revolutionary era, Methodism's commitment to anti-slavery remained strong at first, preachers threatening slaveholders with excommunication if their slaves were not freed. The early years of the nineteenth century, however, saw the Methodist leadership start to accommodate slave ownership. They did not want to damage the Church's appeal at a time when numbers in the South were growing impressively. Methodism, indeed, was particularly popular among wealthy Southern slaveholders who, attracted by its evangelical dimension, began to play an ever-larger role in Church affairs. The question of slavery was relegated from a moral issue to a private matter between master and slave. Southern ministers were even allowed to keep slaves. At the same time, many Methodists in the North continued to denounce slavery, with several ministers actively involved in the Underground Railroad. These tensions between Methodists in the North and South eventually led to schism and the foundation of the Methodist Episcopal Church South in the mid-1840s.

Methodism was not the only religious denomination to struggle with administering to such culturally divergent parts of the same country — Presbyterians and Baptists endured similar schisms. It was, however, the Church closest to Douglass's heart, and consequently the one he attacked most vigorously in his famous autobiographical writings.

'His Burning Eloquence'

The author, a stern-looking young black man, is dressed in a crisp three-piece suit; his hands gloved and a cravat tied loosely around a high-collared white shirt. His wavy hair, combed to one side in a rather futile attempt to quell its natural urge to rise, casts a shadow over the left side of his face. It is his eyes, however, intense and resolute, that are the most striking feature of the portrait, staring out from the frontispiece of *Narrative of the Life of Frederick Douglass, an American Slave*.

Written during the early months of 1845, *Narrative of the Life of Frederick Douglass* — an incendiary autobiographical work destined to become one of the classics of American literature — was Douglass's response to the increased questioning of the authenticity of his story. 'People doubted if I had ever been a slave. They said I did not talk like a slave, look like a slave, nor act like a slave, and they believed I had never been south of Mason and Dixon's line.' An avid reader by now of Byron, Burns, Shakespeare, Milton and Emerson, he did not conform to the common view of an escaped slave. How could a man who claimed to have never had a day's schooling speak so powerfully and eloquently? Even abolitionists had suggested he keep 'a *little* of the plantation' in his stage manner. Douglass, however, refused to play the role of the plantation stooge. He dressed formally and would not disguise the rich voice that even Covey had admired, forcing Douglass to lead the singing at prayer time.

Published by the American Anti-Slavery Society in Boston in the summer of 1845, *Narrative* was an immediate bestseller, a work of art as well as a powerful anti-slavery tract. While far from the first slave narrative to have been printed, it was the best written and most precise in detail, mixing scenes of great emotional warmth with brutal outrages that shocked many readers, Thomas Auld, for instance, pictured quoting Luke 12:47 — 'He who knoweth his master's will, and doeth not, shall be beaten with many stripes' — as he whipped the back of Douglass's disabled cousin Henny. Douglass had revealed his own name together with those of his masters, opening up the possibility of recapture. He had been aware of this danger but, as one of the most prominent black speakers in the country, had felt compelled to act, believing any failure to confront the suspicions surrounding his past would prove fatal to his work in the anti-slavery cause.

The *Narrative* received great praise in the Northern press. It was 'unspeakably affecting', and an 'excellent piece of writing' (*New York Tribune*), an 'extraordinary performance' (*Boston Transcript*), the 'most thrilling work which the American press ever issued — *and the most important*' (*Lynn Pioneer*). 'Frederick is a strong man, and will not fail to arouse the sympathies of his readers on behalf of the oppressed,' wrote the *Practical Christian*. 'May he live long with his burning eloquence, to pour truth on the naked conscience of this wicked nation.' The reaction in the South, however, was one of outrage, the whole book denounced as a 'catalogue of lies' in the *Delaware Republican*.

Anticipating the furore that the publication of the *Narrative* would cause, Garrison and his fellow Boston abolitionists decided to send Douglass on a year-long speaking and fund-raising tour of Great Britain and Ireland. This was a well-worn path for American abolition-ists, the anti-slavery communities on both sides of the Atlantic having long drawn succour from each other. He would stop in Ireland first, where Garrison arranged to have the *Narrative* published by his friend Richard D. Webb, the Dublin Quaker printer who had hosted Remond a few years earlier, even bringing him on holiday to the west coast of County Clare, where the soberly dressed Quaker and dark-skinned stranger walking along the cliffs were a source of amusement for the Irish-speaking locals, especially the children.

Webb and his family were at the heart of a small but well-connected anti-slavery lobby in Ireland. Garrison had met them at the World Anti-Slavery Convention in the summer of 1840, the friendship sealed when Webb and the other Dublin delegates (mainly his relatives) joined Garrison in protesting against the exclusion of women from the main body of the conference hall. (The conference had been organised by the British and Foreign Anti-Slavery Society, who were not quite as advanced when it came to women's rights as slavery.) Garrison spent three days at Webb's home soon afterwards. 'That visit to Dublin!' he exulted to Webb's wife, Hannah, several years later. 'To be so cordially entertained by strangers, being a 'foreigner' [myself] — to be welcomed to their firesides and their hearts . . . my heart has ever since . . . been welling over with the crystal waters of gratitude.'

According to Webb's son Alfred, Webb was 'the best friend and most active worker the anti-slavery cause had on this side of the Atlantic'. Webb wrote articles for the anti-slavery papers in America, organised their distribution among subscribers in Ireland and opened up his home to an array of abolitionists including Garrison, Remond and Henry C. Wright. The latter, a well-known pacifist and as well as an abolitionist who had shared platforms with Douglass in America, would actually spend months at a time locked away in a room of Webb's house, writing pamphlets and books in between lecture tours of Britain and Ireland. Webb was also central to the gathering together of donations from Britain and Ireland for the annual Boston Bazaar, an important American Anti-Slavery Society fundraiser held just before Christmas, the house on Dublin's Great Brunswick Street (present-day Pearse Street) filling up with box-loads of handmade purses, bags, pincushions, scarves, gloves, clothing, ornaments and toys each November. Even the children were involved, Webb's daughter Deborah knitting little wool bags to be shipped across the Atlantic, the overseas items always fetching the highest prices at the Bazaar.

Douglass would travel on board the *Cambria*, one of the then recently established Cunard Line's transatlantic steamships. He was accompanied by James Buffum, a 38-year-old white abolitionist from Lynn, Massachusetts, who had earlier helped Douglass fight a mob throwing him off a train on the Eastern Railroad. Buffum has been treated rather condescendingly in many works, labelled an 'enterprising but slow-thinking carpenter whose means permitted him to indulge a taste for abolitionism' and a 'wealthy, if slightly insipid, Garrisonian from Lynn'. This hardly does justice to a man who after being one of the earliest subscribers to *The Liberator* in 1831 was still working to help freed slaves in the 1870s. And besides, most people would look slightly insipid when measured against the intellectually and physically powerful Douglass. The Hutchinsons, a famous musical family with a strong activist streak, were also on board. Jesse (manager and songwriter), John W., Judson, Asa and Abby had actually shared the stage with Douglass on a number of occasions in the past, working up the crowds with their anti-slavery songs before he launched into his talks.

Genuinely afraid of being 'spirited away' by slave catchers, Douglass was happy to go along with Garrison's plan, if anxious about leaving his family for so long. He had actually been thinking about just such a trip for several months, exhausted in body and mind by the relentless lecturing across New England and the Midwest, but also excited at the prospect of speaking before an international audience. The tour would surpass all Douglass's expectations, although there would be some difficulties along the way.

3

'Safe in Old Ireland'

Built in Scotland in 1844, the *Cambria* was the latest addition to the Cunard Line's Boston-Liverpool transatlantic mail route. It was a 219-ft-long wooden paddle steamer, able to complete in under two weeks a journey that a short time previously had taken more than a month. The *Cambria* had room for about 120 people, but with a focus on the delivery of the mails, and most of the space allocated to engines and coal, passengers and their comforts were something of an after-thought, as Charles Dickens had discovered travelling on another Cunard ship, the *Britannia*, a few years earlier.

The 27-year-old Douglass boarded the *Cambria* on 16 August 1845. He had a first-class ticket but never saw the inside of his cabin, relegated to steerage on account of his colour. Buffum went with him in solidarity. Determined to make the most of the voyage, Douglass and Buffum paid little heed to the conditions in the part of the ship usually reserved for the poorest travellers.

Instead, Douglass recalled fondly how the Hutchinsons often came down 'to my rude forecastle deck and [sang] their sweetest songs, enlivening the place with eloquent music as well as spirited conversation'. The Hutchinsons, who became friendly with the ship's captain, a 'bluff old sterling Englishman' named Charles Judkins, also ensured that Douglass was allowed onto the promenade deck each morning, which despite his stoicism must have been a welcome break from life amidships. He could take the sea breeze, watch icebergs float past and marvel at the wide array of passengers on board. There were doctors, lawyers, soldiers and sailors, a 'scheming Connecticut wooden clockmaker' and a 'large, surly New York lion-tamer', Catholic bishops, Protestant ministers and Quakers, government officials from Canada, a diplomat from Spain and slaveholders from Cuba and Georgia. He also talked slavery to anyone who would listen as the ship made its way across to Ireland, selling copies of his *Narrative* in full view of disgruntled Americans.

'I shall never forget the thrill of pleasure and excitement, the eager rush of passengers from cabin to deck, when ... it was announced by some keen-eyed mariner that the shores of Ireland were in sight,' wrote

Douglass of the evening of 26 August. 'Our voyage had been a pleasant one and the ocean had been more than kind and gentle to us; but whatever may be the character of a voyage, rough or smooth, long or short, the sight of land, after three thousand miles of sea, ship and sky, is unspeakably grateful to the eye and heart of the voyager.' The 'Emerald Isle', as Douglass called it, was even clearer the next morning, the ragged coastlines of Kerry, Cork and Waterford all coming into view. 'Oh, the dear spot where I was born!' exclaimed one passenger from Philadelphia.

That evening, Captain Judkins, acting on a suggestion of the Hutchinsons, invited Douglass to deliver a speech on slavery on the quarterdeck. The ship's bell was sounded and a large number of the passengers gathered around. Judkins introduced Douglass before sneaking away to his cabin to sleep off the champagne he had been sharing with the first-class passengers at the traditional captain's dinner on the last night of a voyage. The Hutchinsons sang an anti-slavery song and Douglass began to speak, quoting some slave laws from Georgia. 'That's a lie,' called one of the passengers as soon as he had finished his first sentence. Douglass tried again. The hecklers, however, led by a

Connecticut man named Hazzard, became more violent, more insulting. 'Down with the nigger,' one shouted. 'He shan't speak,' yelled another. 'Oh, I wish I had you in Cuba,' said a third. Other listeners, including an Irish soldier, Captain Thomas Gough of the 33rd Foot (the Duke of Wellington's regiment), encouraged him to continue. It was not long before the whole scene verged on riot, with passengers who half an hour previously had been drinking each other's health now shouting furiously into each other's faces and clenching their fists. Eventually, Douglass gave up, disappearing back down into steerage. The arguing went on without him, one passenger threatening to throw 'the damned nigger overboard'.

Captain Judkins was woken by an aide and returned to the deck. Order finally restored, the *Cambria* sailed up the Irish Sea, docking in Liverpool on Thursday morning, 28 August. The Hutchinsons set off on a music tour while Douglass and Buffum explored the city. Two days later, the *Cambria* carried the American abolitionists across to Dublin, the cramped and crowded city of almost a quarter of a million souls that would be their home for the next six weeks. They arrived early on Sunday morning, making their way past the liquor shops that surrounded the docks to a warm welcome at the home of James H. Webb, a younger brother of the temporarily absent Richard D. Webb.

A few days later, they were ensconced in the house above the bookshop and printing business at 177 Great Brunswick Street (through the site of which a railway now runs). Douglass was right in the heart of the city, close to Trinity College Dublin around whose walls small bookstands vied for attention with women selling fruit. He was also just a short walk away from the old Irish parliament where, fifty years earlier, Arthur O'Connor had made the speech on Catholic emancipation that so impressed him in *The Columbian Orator*. The parliament, however, once so central to the city's sense of fashion and political importance, was no more, abolished by the Act of Union of 1801, the long centuries of British rule taking new shape in the creation of the United Kingdom of Great Britain and Ireland. Its magnificent home on College Green had become a bank's headquarters, the old House of Commons gutted to make way for clerks and counters, men waiting around outside ready to hold horses as riders alighted.

Douglass had already sent his first dispatch back to America.

'A Kind Providence'

'Dear Friend Garrison: Thanks to a kind Providence, I am now safe in old Ireland, in the beautiful city of Dublin.' These were the first words Douglass sent from Ireland, in a letter to William Lloyd Garrison dated 1 September 1845. It was the first in a series of letters charting Douglass's progress around the country that would find their way into the pages of *The Liberator*. The traveller seemed content, 'surrounded by the kind family and seated at the table of our mutual friend James H. Webb, brother of the well-known Richard D. Webb'. His mind, however, was still full of the remarkable events on board the *Cambria*, a mix of righteous indignation and nervous energy coursing through his words.

'I know it will gladden your heart to hear that from the moment we first lost sight of the American shore, till we landed at Liverpool, our gallant steam-ship was the theatre of an almost constant discussion of the subject of slavery — commencing cool, but growing hotter every moment as it advanced,' Douglass began. 'It was a great time for anti-slavery, and a hard time for slavery; the one delighting in the sunshine of free discussion, and the other horror-stricken at its God-like approach.' Turning to events on the last night of the crossing, he wrote

71

incredulously how the pro-slavery passengers 'actually got up a *mob* — a real American, republican, democratic, Christian mob' when he was invited to deliver a lecture on deck. 'The clamour went on long after I ceased speaking, and was only silenced by the captain, who told the mobocrats if they did not cease their clamour, he would have them put in irons; and he actually sent for the irons, and doubtless would have made use of them, had not the rioters become orderly.'

'Such is but a faint outline of an AMERICAN MOB ON BOARD OF A BRITISH STEAM PACKET,' the escaped slave concluded, leaving any thoughts on the city he had just arrived in to later letters.

'A Tale of Woe'
The Dublin Douglass arrived in was a city in decline, the wealth and grandeur of its late eighteenth-century pomp giving way to extreme poverty and decay. The loss of its parliament had been a severe blow to its prestige. Pollution and sickness were rife. The economy, too, was in a desperate way, with many traditional, labour-intensive industries like cotton and silk close to collapse. The day before Douglass's arrival, a number of newspapers had carried an appeal for funds from the Sick and Indigent

Roomkeepers' Society, one of the longest-established charities in the city. Many of the applicants for relief, the appeal read, were 'respectable tradesmen out of employment', who, 'being ashamed to beg', hid 'themselves in the cheerless garret, and deep cellars, with their helpless children, where they anticipate the indescribable misery of starvation'.

The scene was not unremittingly bleak, as Dublin remained an important commercial city as well as the centre of Irish law, learning and medicine. It had an active stock exchange and provided the natural home for the Irish headquarters of large British companies, especially insurance companies. Dublin Castle, the beating heart of the British administration in Ireland, was still the scene of glittering balls and stylish soirées. Nevertheless, the sense of a city being abandoned to its poor, its wretched and infirm was unmistakeable, with many of the leading aristocratic families having long since decamped for London — their fashionable homes on the north side of the city falling into tenement use. The remaining gentry and affluent middle classes, meanwhile, had started to move out to the new suburbs like Rathmines.

Within days of arriving, Douglass was taken on a tour of the city by 'a gentleman of great respectability'. Other outings took him to Dalkey and a cliff-top walk around Howth Head. Douglass appreciated the fine architectural beauty of public buildings such as the Four Courts and the Custom House. He also believed a number of the main business streets in the city bore favourable comparison with those of New York and Philadelphia. Douglass was particularly impressed with Sackville Street (present-day O'Connell Street). 'It is broad, straight, far-reaching and grand. It is lined on either side with fine stores, laden with the riches of all lands and languages.' It was not long, however, before the less savoury sides of the city came to his attention, the legions of poor sidling up to the tall, well-dressed black man in search of spare change.

'The streets were . . . alive with beggars displaying the greatest wretchedness,' Douglass wrote to Garrison, 'some of them mere stumps of men, without feet, without legs, without hands, without arms — and others still more horribly deformed, with crooked limbs, down upon their hands and knees, their feet lapped around each other, and laid upon their backs, pressing their way through the muddy streets and merciless crowd, casting sad looks to the right and left, in the hope of catching the eye of a passing stranger — the citizens generally having set their faces against giving to beggars.' He continued:

I have had more than a dozen around me at one time, men, women and children, all telling a tale of woe which would move any but a heart of iron. Women, barefooted and bareheaded, and only covered by rags which seemed to be held together by the very dirt and filth with which they were covered — many of these had infants in their arms, whose emaciated forms, sunken eyes and pallid cheeks told too plainly that they had nursed till they had nursed in vain. In such a group you may hear all forms of appeal, entreaty and expostulation. A half a dozen voices have broken upon my ear at once: 'Will your honour please to give me a penny to buy some bread?' 'May the Lord bless you, give the poor old woman a little sixpence.' 'For the love of God, leave us a few pennies — we will divide them amongst us.' 'Oh! my poor child, it must starve, for God's sake give me a penny.' 'More power to you! I know your honour will leave the poor creature something. Ah, do! Ah, do! And I will pray for you as long as I live.'

For a time, Douglass 'gave way' to his feelings, doling out change to the city's poor. He was advised to stop, however, told that he could empty his pockets every day without making a dent in the number of beggars in the city. Douglass complied. 'I fear it had a hardening effect upon my heart, as I found it much easier to pass without giving to the last beggar than the first.'

Douglass also went walking in the Dublin Hills with his new Irish associates — a painful experience that made clear the stark reality of life for the majority of the 8 million inhabitants of the island. Three decades of severe economic distress, dating back to the end of the Napoleonic Wars, had taken a heavy toll, and an Irish hut, Douglass declared, was the pre-eminent place in the world to observe 'human misery, ignorance, degradation, filth and wretchedness'. He described one to Garrison: four mud walls about six feet high, thatched with straw, a mud chimney at one end, no divisions of any kind on the inside, no real floor, no windows, a piece of pine board laid on the top of a box or an old chest, a pile of straw covered with dirty clothes, a tattered picture of the crucifixion, a few broken dishes stuck up in a corner, an iron pot in one corner of the chimney and a little peat in the fireplace 'aggravating one occasionally with a glimpse of fire . . . but sending out very little heat'. In this squalor lived a man, his wife, five or so children — and a pig.

Similar scenes had been witnessed by other foreign travellers to the country in the 1830s and 1840s, from the German travel writer Johann Kohl to the English novelist William Makepeace Thackeray, the cumulative effect of their words making Ireland a byword for poverty the world over. However, it was not the huts of the poor or the beggars in the city that affected Douglass the most, but the sight of so many young children in the streets late at night, 'covered with filthy rags, and seated upon cold stone steps, or in corners, leaning against brick walls, fast asleep, with none to look upon them, none to care for them ... Poor creatures! They are left without help, to find their way through a frowning world — a world that seems to regard them as intruders, and to be punished as such.'

'Where is your religion that takes care for the poor — for the widow and fatherless — where are its votaries — what are they doing?' Douglass asked. His answer — 'wasting their energies in useless debate on hollow creeds and points of doctrine, which, when settled, neither make one hair white nor black' — bore the mark of a man with a deep distrust of organised religions, most of whom seemed to his mind more concerned with looking after their own interests than pursuing God's work. Some pious priests and ministers even quoted passages from the Bible to explain away their lack of action: Deuteronomy 15:11 — 'The poor shall not cease out of the land.'

Douglass's hostility to the established religions would be a regular feature of his talks in Ireland, as would the possibility of war across the Atlantic and what it meant for the expansion of slavery.

'The Files of American Journals'
The arrival of the *Cambria* had been eagerly awaited by the Dublin press. Their chief interest, however, lay not in the escaped-slave-turned-orator travelling on board but rather the prospect of war between America and Mexico. 'From what is contained in the files of American journals which we have received . . . we are led to anticipate the breaking out of hostilities between the United States and Mexico,' reported *The Freeman's Journal*, which printed extracts from papers including the *New York Herald* and the New Orleans *Picayune* alongside an editorial on the subject. Long-standing tensions between the countries had been brought to a head earlier in the year by the American annexation of slave-owning Texas (an independent republic since 1836 when it won independence from Mexico). The papers were slightly premature in their

predictions as war was not actually declared until May 1846. The fighting would last almost two years, American victory adding half a million square miles — including the present-day states of California, Nevada, Utah and New Mexico — to its territory.

Other items in that day's *Freeman's Journal* included an advertisement for the Ship Tavern, 5 Lower Abbey Street, where 'Gentlemen may dine on a variety of the Primest Joints for one shilling each . . . from five to seven o'clock each day'. As an added attraction, 'Quinn, the celebrated Irish Harper', also performed there each evening. Under the heading 'Board and Education for Young Ladies', a woman informed readers that she could accommodate 'Two or Three Young Ladies as Boarders, where they can finish their Education in every polite and useful accomplishment, consisting of French, Italian, Music, Drawing, &c, in a Private Family, on Moderate Terms'. There was a notice for an auction at 7 Rathmines Terrace of the extensive effects of 'the late Frederick Howard, Esq.'. Still in the 'best state of preservation', these included 'seven elaborately-carved Antique Chairs, covered with needle-work', a 'handsome Rosewood Loo Table', 'Grecian Sofas and Couches', 'Feather Beds, Bolsters and Pillows' and a panoply of dressers, wardrobes, bookcases, blankets and carpets. Jobs, too, were being advertised, despite the poor economic situation, with an experienced flour miller required at one company and an 'accomplished' Catholic lady needed to work as a governess.

There was also a report of a talk given by a Thomas George Tilly to the Royal Zoological Society of Ireland, and an advertisement for the rather more intriguing-sounding 'experimental' lecture by Thomas Adair on mesmerism and phreno-mesmerism, new therapeutic techniques involving hypnotism. A few days later a local surgeon named Mathias would give a rival talk on the absurdities of phreno-mesmerism. Public lectures of this kind were extremely popular in mid-nineteenth-century Ireland, and not just with the upper and middle classes. Throughout the country Mechanics' Institutes, Athenaeums and Literary and Scientific Societies — all boasting their own small libraries, museums and laboratories — opened up new worlds of culture and science to their artisan and working-class members.

It is no surprise, therefore, that the young orator Douglass was thrust quickly onto the stage.

'Anti-Everythingarians'
'The great attraction of the evening was Mr Frederick Douglass, an American of colour,

who was but a few years ago a slave,' wrote *The Freeman's Journal*, the newspaper of record for the time, in a short notice of his first major speech in Ireland. The setting for the talk, delivered to the monthly meeting of the Hibernian Anti-Slavery Society on the evening of Wednesday 3 September, was a lecture room in the magnificent Royal Exchange on Dame Street (the present-day City Hall). Douglass was introduced by his short, stout and slightly balding forty-year-old Quaker host, Webb, a founder member of the society in 1837.

The Hibernian Anti-Slavery Society had grown out of a number of the smaller anti-slavery groups that emerged in Ireland in the late 1820s and 1830s during the push to abolish slavery in the British West Indies. The Quaker element in the society was strong. In fact, it had been a Quaker, Mary Peisley from Kildare, who really introduced anti-slavery thinking into Ireland, publishing a pamphlet condemning Quaker slaveholders, after visiting North Carolina in the 1750s. The connection between Irish Quakers and their American brethren was always close, with family letters constantly crossing the Atlantic and Irish Quakers investing in land in Pennsylvania. It is no surprise, therefore, that as the eighteenth century progressed some

Irish Quakers followed their American counterparts in campaigning against slavery — publishing poems, pamphlets and books that revealed the sufferings of transported Africans on American plantations. They were also heavily involved in the campaign to boycott slave-produced goods like sugar in the 1790s. Indeed, it was soon said that the only two engravings commonly found in Quaker homes were 'Penn's Peace with the Indians' and a diagrammatic section of a slave ship showing the appalling cramped conditions of the chained slaves held on board.

The first recorded Quaker meeting in Ireland took place at the home of an English-born shopkeeper named William Edmundson in Lurgan, County Armagh, in 1654. This was just a few years after the group's young English founder, George Fox, one of the myriad charismatic mystics and visionaries to emerge out of the chaos and upheaval of the English Civil Wars, started preaching in public about the 'Inner Light' that was the path to a full relationship with God. At first, Fox and his followers had been known as the Children of Light, the Friends of Truth or simply Friends; the name Quaker derived from an incident in which Fox told a judge to tremble at the name of the Lord. Like many other early Quakers in England,

Fox would spend a great deal of time before the courts and in prisons. They were seen as subversives and blasphemers, undesirables in a country still coming to terms with decades of social and political turmoil. They had no clergy, liturgy or sacraments, believing instead in the primacy of the Spirit and direct communication with God. Although non-violent, they were imbued with what one writer has termed a 'spiritual militancy', bursting into churches in the middle of services to excoriate the shallowness and hypocrisy of the established religions. They also refused to pay tithes or take oaths, Fox finding no justification for either in the Bible. They even allowed women and children to speak at the religious gatherings — called simply 'meetings' — in which they congregated.

The Quakers in Ireland were just as radical at first, Edmundson, for example, a former soldier in Oliver Cromwell's New Model Army, nailing his 'Truth' to the doors of churches in the north of the country. They were just as persecuted, too, attacked by Protestant worshippers, banished from towns, beaten up by soldiers and thrown into jail on the slightest pretext. Despite these early difficulties, the Quakers established themselves as a presence in the country, growing less confrontational and more inward-looking over the years. They developed a stark, rather puritan air, dressing simply, using 'thee' and 'thou' and keeping to their businesses, their Bibles and their near-silent, communal worship. To the bewilderment of the Catholic masses, they refused to celebrate feast days like Christmas or Easter or participate in frivolous entertainments like music or dance. Nevertheless, they gained respect for their honesty and integrity in business and generosity in times of crisis. This reputation for fair dealing and charity was still strong by the time Douglass arrived in the country. Not everyone, however, saw them in so pure a light, one disgruntled ex-member, Sarah Greer, writing a book in the early 1850s that portrayed the Quakers (in the words of the aristocratic diarist Elizabeth Smith) as 'a set of cold, worldly-minded, purse-proud, selfish, sensual, indolent, stupid, ignorant, immoral human beings'.

Alongside Webb, other important members of the Hibernian Anti-Slavery Society included Richard Allen and James Haughton. Allen was a 42-year-old Quaker with his own tailoring and drapery store in Dublin city. Haughton, about a decade older, owned a successful flour-milling business with his brother. He had been born into a Quaker family but joined the Unitarians. As children, Webb and Haughton had attended the famous Quaker school in Ballitore, County Kildare, imbibing the anti-slavery spirit of the schoolmaster Richard Shackleton, a forebear of the famous explorer Ernest Shackleton. They were now with Allen, soberly dressed, high-minded men, easily recognised on the streets of the city. Dubbed 'Anti-Everythingarians' by the *Dublin Evening Mail*, they campaigned on a number of causes besides slavery, including temperance, pacifism, prison reform and the abolition of capital punishment. Their beliefs permeated the lives of their children, Webb's son Alfred describing how he and his siblings were overheard playing with their toys and dolls: 'Now thee is going to a slavery meeting; now thee is going to a temperance meeting.'

Shortly after the formation of the Hibernian Anti-Slavery Society, Allen, whose deep and distracting involvement in so many philanthropic adventures almost cost him his business, travelled to London with James H. Webb and Edward Baldwin, another member of the society, to present the young Queen Victoria with a petition signed by 75,000 Irish women calling for an end to the 'apprenticeship' system that had succeeded slavery in the West Indies. This was part of a broader campaign against apprenticeship (slavery in all but name) spearheaded by the British and Foreign Anti-Slavery Society. The campaign was successful and apprenticeship was abolished in May 1838. Prior to meeting the Queen, the Irish Quakers had to have their hats removed by attendants. Allen also recalled that when it came to kissing the Queen's hand, he, 'contrary to custom', had remained straight-backed, raising her hand to his lips, such actions recalling the early days of Quakerism, when Fox's belief in the 'Inner Light' combined with an anti-authoritarian stance that saw Quakers refuse to doff their hats to social superiors.

A few years later, Webb, Allen and Haughton helped write the 'Address of the Irish People to Their Countrymen and Countrywomen in America', a famous document carrying 60,000 signatures that encouraged (unsuccessfully) Irish Americans to unite with the abolitionists. Brought across the Atlantic by Charles Lenox Remond, the Irish Address was unveiled before a mass meeting at Boston's Faneuil Hall in January 1842. Douglass was in attendance as it was read out. 'What a spectacle does America present to the earth!' the address declared. 'A land of professing Christian republicans, uniting their energies for the oppression of three millions of innocent human beings, the children of one common

Father.' Rather than embrace America in its current state, the address called upon Irish Americans to treat black men and women as their equals. 'By all your memories of Ireland,' it concluded passionately, 'continue to love liberty — hate slavery — CLING BY THE ABOLITIONISTS — and in America you will do honour to the name of Ireland.'

The Irish Address was supported by Daniel O'Connell and Fr Theobald Mathew, the famous temperance leader. Their imprimatur, however, did not turn anti-slavery into anything approaching a mass movement in Ireland, and at the time of Douglass's arrival it remained what it had always been: a small, mainly Nonconformist Protestant crusade. Nevertheless, the Catholic majority were not totally disengaged, the weekly meetings of the Hibernian Anti-Slavery Society often full of what Webb described as the city's 'ragamuffins'. Although more interested in learning about America in general — already imprinted on many minds as a potential destination — than anti-slavery, they were always, Webb wrote, the 'heartiest clappers'. They were certainly present as Douglass stepped onto the stage of the Royal Exchange, word of mouth alone ensuring the lecture room was crowded to excess with many others turned away.

Douglass had come to Ireland 'to plead the cause of the oppressed black man', *The Freeman's Journal* observed, assuring him of 'a hearty welcome'. He spoke for about forty-five minutes, describing slavery as a system 'which made a chattel of a man . . . which tore the husband and wife asunder . . . and which deprived men of all their rights as human beings'. Perhaps in part to win favour with his Irish audience, but also from genuine admiration, one of his first comments had concerned O'Connell. 'When he spoke of O'Connell as the admired of all who loved liberty and hated oppression the world over,' the paper noted, 'the assembly rose and expressed their hearty approval of the noble course pursued by the Liberator in several rounds of applause.' Douglass was followed on stage by Buffum, who spoke briefly and was also warmly received. Webb was next to speak, making a 'solemn and beautiful' appeal to the audience 'as Irishmen, as patriots, and as true lovers of liberty, to be consistent advocates of freedom, and to spurn with contempt the sympathy of the guilty slave-holder'. It was left to the remorselessly pure Haughton to bring matters to a close, exhorting the large crowd to give up tobacco, a slave-grown product, 'for the sake of the poor, oppressed black man'.

And so, Douglass's first anti-slavery speech in Ireland was brought to an end — a small but significant affair.

4

'A Total Absence of Prejudice'

'Our success here is even greater than I had anticipated,' a delighted Frederick Douglass wrote to William Lloyd Garrison in mid-September 1845. 'We have held four glorious anti-slavery meetings — two in the Royal Exchange and two in the Friends Meeting House — all crowded to overflowing.' Douglass's greatest pleasure, however, came not from the success of his lectures, but rather the manner in which he was treated on the street. 'One of the most pleasing features of my visit . . . has been a total absence of . . . prejudice against me on account of my colour. The change of circumstances, in this, is particularly striking. I go on stage coaches, omnibuses, steamboats, into the first cabins and in the first public houses without seeing the slightest manifestation of that hateful and vulgar feeling against me. I find myself not treated as a *colour*, but as a *man* — not as a thing, but as a child of the common Father of us all.'

Dubliners were used to the sight of black men and women on the streets, be they servants, soldiers or sailors. (Black singers and actors also performed regularly on the capital's stages.) The numbers were small, no more than a few hundred at any one time, but this was still enough to give Dublin a larger black population than almost any European city other than London. The black presence in Ireland spread further still, to other port cities like Cork and Belfast and even Longford, Mayo and Donegal. Occasionally, a newspaper article might describe a crowd of white people staring strangely at a black mother and child. For the most part, however, their presence was unremarkable. They certainly do not appear to have been subjected to any widespread racist abuse, newspapers accounts of mixed-race marriages or parties where black men danced with white women containing no hint of reproach. This would not have been the case in Douglass's homeland of the American South.

Nevertheless, Ireland's relationship with slavery and the slave trade was far from unblemished, for although slavery as an institution had largely disappeared from the British Isles by the late 1500s, small numbers of slaves were still being held up to the mid-1700s. They may not have been subjected to anything like the terrible conditions of slaves in the Caribbean, Brazil or the American South but they were still denied the same rights as their white owners — still referred to and seen as property. 'A Negro Boy and Slave, called Brazill, the property of William Nicholson, Esq., has been missing since Thursday evening last,' ran one notice in a Dublin paper in the 1750s. 'Run away from the service of Mrs Fullerton of Carrickfergus, on Sunday last, a negro slave boy,' read another. Prominent Irish families owned slave estates in the West Indies, and Antoine Walsh from Kilkenny was just one example of an Irishman amassing a fortune in the French slave trade. Even Daniel O'Connell's famous claim that no slave ship had ever left Ireland's shores to ply the 'odious traffic' was mistaken. They may have been illegal, but they certainly existed, the last recorded Irish slave ship, a brigantine, the *Prosperity* from Limerick, sailing into Barbados on 31 July 1718 with ninety-six slaves aboard.

Many Irish merchants also got rich supplying the British, French and Dutch islands of the Caribbean with provisions — the islands themselves focused solely on the production of their cash crops (sugar, cotton, indigo and coffee). The port of Cork, in particular, owed much of its success in the eighteenth century to this trade, devising special techniques to ensure the preservation of its beef, butter and fish in high temperatures. The better-quality meat went straight to the plates of the planters while the slaves made do with 'cow beef', the carcasses of elderly dairy cattle, specially fattened and cut up into small pieces. Belfast, too, had strong links with the Caribbean, supplying, for example, the coarse linen and shoes with which planters clothed their slaves. Some of these Irish merchants, like the Blakes from Galway and Creaghs from Limerick, went on to settle in the Caribbean as merchants, planters and slaveholders, a David Creagh purchasing a plantation in Barbados in the early 1700s, equipping it with more than 200 slaves bought for about £25 a head.

A few merchants even tried to get the country more directly involved in the slave trade, with a plan announced for the establishment of an 'African company' in Limerick in 1784. Six ships would be employed annually, carrying firearms, linen, cottons, soap, candles and even 'Dutch toys' to the slave coast of West Africa where in true triangular-trade style they would be exchanged for hundreds of slaves who would in turn be traded in the West Indies for sugar, coffee and other tropically grown goods. A similar proposal was mooted for Belfast a year later. Neither venture, however, took off, in part because of growing anti-slavery sentiment. 'May God eternally damn the soul of the man who subscribes the first guinea,' wrote the radial watchmaker and United Irishman, Thomas McCabe, of the Belfast plan.

And so, instead of helping carry ever more African slaves across the Atlantic to lives of suffering and bondage, Ireland was soon playing host to a wide array of anti-slavery speakers, from the freed slave Olaudah Equiano in the 1790s to Charles Lenox Remond, Douglass and others some fifty years later.

'Some Entirely Groundless Huff'

'Free Admission', 'No Collection', the advertisements for Douglass's second lecture to a Dublin crowd had promised, his anti-slavery backers trying to build up as much interest as possible in their guest speaker. The tactic worked: the Quaker Meeting House in Eustace Street in central Dublin was 'crowded in every part by a most respectable and attentive audience' on the evening of Tuesday 9 September. It was another encouraging affair, Douglass's urging of the audience to make 'every American slaveholder, every American apologist of slavery, who set his feet upon our soil — *feel* that he was in a land of freedom, among a people that hated oppression, and who loved liberty — liberty for all; for the black man as well as the white man — to make them feel that they breathed in a pure anti-slavery air' eliciting such loud applause he had to ask for quiet on account of the sombre nature of the venue.

Douglass had made an immediate impact on the city and his kind reception on the streets was matched in the pages of the capital's press, *The Freeman's Journal, Dublin Evening Mail* and other papers praising his 'cultivated mind' and 'manly and eloquent' speeches. He was certainly getting a lot of column inches, even though his arrival coincided with a number of other major news stories, including the death of Thomas Davis, the young nationalist poet and editor of *The Nation*. 'Frederick is very popular here,' James Buffum wrote back to Boston, regretting that they had not carried over more copies of *The Liberator* and anti-slavery pamphlets like Theodore Dwight Weld's *American Slavery As It Is*, a devastating documentation of the cruelties inflicted by the 'peculiar institution' assembled from the testimony of a thousand eyewitnesses (some former slaveholders), state legal codes and the South's own newspapers accounts and advertisements. The 'people', Buffum continued, were 'very anxious to learn' about slavery, the crowded nature of the meetings at the Royal Exchange and the Quaker Meeting House meaning larger venues would soon be required. Nevertheless, Douglass's first weeks in Ireland had not been without some moments of awkwardness and controversy.

Douglass was back at the Meeting House on Friday 12 September (the night after his second speech at the Royal Exchange). It was this talk that caused difficulties, a coruscating attack on the Methodist Church, which embarrassed the Dublin Quakers and got him banned from the Meeting House. Webb, apparently, had spent much of the meeting running around trying to quieten down Catholics in the audience taking too much noisy delight at the Methodists being so roundly chastised.

Douglass had been thrilled and surprised when Richard D. Webb arranged use of the Meeting House, remembering how he had been locked out of similar venues in America. 'Only think of our holding a meeting in the *Meeting House* of the Society of Friends!' he had written Garrison, when 'at home they would almost bolt us out of their yards'. Such instances had been pertinent reminders that while many Quakers had strong activist streaks a much more conservative majority looked askance at public agitation. Officially, indeed, the Quakers in America had adopted a wholly moderate anti-slavery stance, opposing abolitionism and immediate emancipation. Douglass's travelling companion Buffum had been one of many Quakers to leave the group on account of this apparent passivity. Others would be expelled. These tensions among Quakers in America had recently come to a head with a divisive split in the Indiana Yearly Meeting, a split caused in large part by the refusal of anti-slavery Quakers to heed the warnings of the Yearly Meeting to stop breaking the law by aiding slaves on the Underground Railroad. Similar tensions were evident in Ireland, Webb fully aware that many co-religionists looked on his activities with suspicion and disdain.

Webb supported Douglass fully in the aftermath of the ban, writing a letter of protest to the Dublin Monthly Meeting. Their own relationship, however, soon started to fray, Webb complaining to Maria Weston Chapman, one of the leading Garrisonians in Boston, about Douglass's rudeness to his cousin Elizabeth (Lizzy) Poole and sister-in-law Maria Waring. 'They are both young women — sensible and comely. They walked with him and talked with him and treated him with respect and kindness and no condescension. Yet for some entirely ground-less huff he took, he treated L.P. in such a contemptuous . . . manner that I was and have ever since been perfectly indignant.'

Not wanting to distract from the effort to

raise the profile of the anti-slavery movement in Ireland, Webb kept his counsel until Douglass left the country. Once unleashed, however, there was no holding back. 'In all my experience of men I have never known one . . . so able and willing as he is to magnify the smallest causes of discomfort . . . into insurmountable hills of offence and dissatisfaction. He is in my opinion . . . the least likable and the least easy of all the abolitionists with whom I have come into intimate association. I think his selfishness intense, his affections weak and his unreasonableness quite extravagant when he is in the slightest degree hurt or when he thinks himself hurt.' Softly spoken in public, Webb clearly had a talent for invective with the pen.

Although such strong criticisms from a man of Webb's moral stature cannot be ignored, it is difficult to reconcile them with the otherwise almost overwhelmingly positive response to Douglass in the country. Webb believed the 'praise and petting' Douglass received in Dublin had gone to his head. It is also possible, however, Douglass got a sense that he was being treated by his Quaker hosts with the kind of condescension he thought he had left behind him in America. 'The ladies had taken their exotic guest out on a leash, for all of Dublin to see. They thought it unseemly when he barked,' Douglass's biographer, William S. McFeely, has observed of the incident with Lizzy Poole and Maria Waring. The fact that Waring would go on to describe him as a 'wild animal' lent credence to Douglass's feeling that something was amiss. Webb's wife, Hannah, meanwhile, would call Douglass 'a child — a savage'. That they did not mean anything harsh by these words merely underlines the impression that he was being looked on in a benign but somewhat racist manner.

Webb, too, seems to have been guilty of some double standards. As with Charles Lenox Remond a few years earlier, he gave Douglass some 'hints' on how to comport himself in the British Isles — the two black men bristling at being told how to act — while visiting white abolitionists like Henry C. Wright received no such 'schooling'. Webb also had form in attacking those whose behaviour did not live up to his standards of gentlemanly conduct, Remond's failure to send back prompt letters of thanks to some of his supporters in Ireland leading Webb to suggest that 'eloquence and not gratitude is Remond's forte'. Webb did not forgive or forget, going on to write of Remond that he had been a 'shameless beggar at times', and that he had 'behaved very often like a big spoiled child'. His break with Douglass would lead to a similarly long-lasting antagonism.

Alert to any hint of patronising behaviour, Douglass may well have been somewhat sharp with his hosts in Dublin. Webb's response, however, was over the top. Indeed, it makes him seem as thin-skinned as he accused Douglass of being. James Haughton was probably somewhere closer to the truth, writing of Douglass: 'He is a fine, manly fellow, but like perhaps most of us, somewhat impatient of reproof.'

None of these quarrels stopped Douglass bringing his anti-slavery message to ever-greater numbers, embarking on the evening of Wednesday 17 September on a series of three hugely successful appearances at the Music Hall in Dublin.

'Mangled With the Lash'
The Music Hall on Lower Abbey Street — home in later years to the Abbey Theatre — was one of the main entertainment venues in mid-nineteenth-century Dublin, playing host to a wide variety of concerts, shows and lectures. It had a capacity of more than 3,000 and was normally let, Douglass told Garrison, for 'about fifty dollars a night'. The mercurial Webb, however, convinced the proprietor John Classon

to donate it to the anti-slavery cause free of charge. Nevertheless, this was the first of Douglass's talks in Dublin to charge an entrance fee — an extremely reasonable 4d to the main body of the house and 2d to the gallery (a concert a few weeks earlier charged 6d for seats in the gallery). The funds were needed to defray expenses incurred by the Hibernian Anti-Slavery Society, including placards and newspaper advertisements. The interest created by Douglass's earlier talks ensured a full house.

Douglass took to the stage at eight o'clock, launching immediately into the story of his life as a slave. Although far from the worst treated of slaves, his back had still been 'mangled with the lash'. Well versed in the art of capturing an audience's attention, he lifted up a whip, some manacles and other instruments of torture used in the slave states, rattling them before the gasp-filled hall. Douglass had carried them across the Atlantic, packed away perhaps in the same suitcase as his shirts and trousers. They would certainly have made an interesting sight for an inquisitive customs official.

Unafraid of controversy, Douglass returned to the question of the American Churches and slavery. 'The word of God had been profaned . . . to the purposes of slavery,' he declared, clergymen in America justifying the flogging of slaves with distorted quotes from the Bible. Almost all the main religious bodies were in some way culpable, Douglass argued, citing Baptists, Congregationalists and Presbyterians. Nevertheless, it was the Methodists who were again his main target. 'The Methodists in America supported slavery, and when he exposed their conduct the other night to their friends in Dublin, he had the door of the Meeting House closed against him . . . But whatever he might incur from them, he would not sacrifice his friends now in chains, and perhaps writhing under the lash while he spoke, to any fear of personal inconvenience . . . While he lived, he would plead for those whom he left behind him in bondage.'

The relentless attacks on American Methodists were part of Douglass's plan to fracture relations between the American Churches and their British and Irish counterparts. He wanted to isolate and ostracise the slaveholding Churches and expose them to the moral glare of international public opinion. It was a valid tactic, the Churches in America genuinely craving respectability in world religious opinion and cherishing the dream of a worldwide Protestant federation. The criticisms certainly discomfited the Methodists in Dublin, many of whom had been to the fore of the efforts to abolish slavery in the West Indies in the early 1830s. The years since, however, had seen the Methodists, like other Protestant denominations in Ireland, grow more cautious in their relationship with anti-slavery, its divisiveness as a subject painfully apparent in the schisms renting the American Churches apart. The Dublin Methodists had consequently refused Remond use of their churches in 1841. They would do the same to Douglass four years later.

Douglass finished his first talk at the Music Hall by asking 'the friends of freedom in this country to test and question the American Methodists or other Christians when they came to Ireland as to whether they supported slavery at home'. It was, he said, 'a fair and plain question to put to them, and the worth of their religious professions would be proved by their answers, supported by their acts'. He then sat down amidst great cheering, tired but exhilarated after an hour and a half on his feet.

He was back on stage a week later.

'Do the Black Man Justice'
Chaired by Dublin's Protestant Lord Mayor, John L. Arabin, Douglass's second Music Hall speech was another ninety-minute affair,

103

melding his life story with more attacks on the hypocrisy of the American Churches, the Quakers this time receiving the brunt of the abuse. The constant talk of religion would not have bored Irish audiences, enmeshed as religion was in every facet of life in the country. The Catholics in the hall would certainly have enjoyed the denunciations of the Protestant denominations, and there were loud cheers when Douglass — conveniently overlooking the fact that its leadership, including many Irish-born bishops, tacitly approved of slavery — declared that of all the Churches in America, only the Roman Catholic Church had never shut its doors to black worshippers. Douglass had also addressed the subject of slave education, demonstrating, in the words of *The Freeman's Journal*, the 'fallacy' of the argument 'so frequently resorted to by slave-holders', that black people were 'unfit for freedom' owing to their 'mental inferiority' to whites. Those that charged slaves 'with being ignorant and degraded condemned themselves in that charge', Douglass argued, 'for they had made education penal, and darkened the understanding of the slave'. American society had 'conspired' against the slaves, seeking 'justification for oppression in the results of that oppression'. He did not want the 'white man to educate the slave or give him office — all he asked was to do the black man justice, and leave him to advance himself'.

The evening had opened with some songs from the Hutchinson Family, who had crossed over to Dublin on board the steamer *Madrid* a few days earlier after three weeks of engagements in Liverpool. Met at the harbour by Buffum and Thomas Webb, they had travelled into the city and taken rooms at the Northumberland Hotel. They gave some concerts of their own at the Music Hall and other venues and spent a good deal of time with Douglass and the Webbs, Allens and Haughtons, singing songs around the tables of the various homes, even though such simple pleasures were something of a 'forbidden article' among Quakers. They had actually travelled over from America with their own letter of introduction from Maria Weston Chapman to Richard Allen, who lived in De Vesci Lodge in Monkstown a few miles outside of the city. The Hutchinsons would stay in Ireland for more than a month, walking the streets, seeing the sights and meeting Daniel O'Connell and Fr Mathew. Abby, a 'charming girl of eighteen' at the time, would return for a short holiday in the 1870s, staying with Webb's son Alfred and reminiscing about the great temperance and anti-slavery days.

Impressed by the speech, Arabin declared himself a 'complete convert' to abolitionism amid loud cheers. He also invited Douglass and Buffum to dine with him at the Mansion House, the official residence of Dublin's Lord Mayors, a few nights later. A number of aldermen and councillors were also present as toasts were drunk to Douglass's health, the teetotal Haughton disapproving strongly of this custom. Douglass delighted in such high-level shows of support for abolitionism. 'What a pity there was not some American democratic Christian at the door of his splendid mansion, to bark out at my approach, 'They don't allow niggers in here!'' Douglass wrote to Garrison, comparing his reception by the Lord Mayor with the resistance met from political leaders in American cities. In fact, he would be keen throughout his travels to show American readers how the elites of Britain and Ireland supported the anti-slavery cause, not mentioning, however, the self-serving nature of some of this support, which allowed 'monarchical' Britain to assume the moral high ground against 'democratic' America.

'Slavery Will Fall to the Ground'
Held on the evening of Wednesday 1 October, Douglass's third and final Music Hall appearance had been promoted for days by

advertisements in the papers, the Hibernian Anti-Slavery Society encouraging Dubliners to take advantage of their last chance to see Douglass in action. The constant attacks on the religious bodies had clearly been troublesome, Haughton, in the chair, feeling compelled to address what he called 'some misconception' of Douglass's views. 'It was undeniable that every section of the church was guilty of the sin of upholding slavery, but that among them all many noble-minded individuals were to be found who were anxious to purge their church from this vile stain. Such men were worthy of all honour; but those who sustain slavery . . . should be held up to the condemnation of mankind. This was all that Mr Douglass meant to convey.'

Douglass then stepped forward, brandishing once again some chains and whips and urging the audience to help 'break the chains which bound the black man in America'. 'I love religion,' he then declared, conscious that he had been portrayed in some quarters as an enemy of religion.

I love the religion of Jesus which is pure and peaceable . . . I ask you all to love this religion . . . but I hate a religion which . . . prostitutes His blessed precepts to the vile purposes of slavery . . . which tears the wife from the husband — which separates the child from the parent — which covers the backs of men and women with bloody scars — which promotes all manner of licentiousness. I hate such a religion as this, for it is not Christianity, it is of the devil. I ask you to hate it too, and to assist me in putting in its place the religion of Jesus.

He continued passionately: 'Let the Methodist minister, the Presbyterian minister, the Baptist minister, the Unitarian minister, the Catholic clergyman and the Protestant clergyman — let the Society of Friends — let all of every denomination in Ireland be faithful to their saviour, and slavery in America will soon fall to the ground.' He believed this because Americans, despite their boasts and bluster, were highly sensitive to the opinion held of them in European countries, particularly Britain and Ireland.

Friends of the poor slave, be therefore firm and faithful in your remonstrances with Americans — let your press teem with denunciations — let your pulpits proclaim to the world that Christianity disavows all fellowship with man-stealers

— let your social circle all talk on the subject as one of deep importance to the interests of humanity — let your entire community be filled with anti-slavery sentiment, so that when slaveholders or apologists of the system visit your country they may feel that they breathe in an atmosphere too pure to be contaminated by them.

'I am the representative of three millions of bleeding slaves,' Douglass concluded evocatively to thunderous applause. 'I have felt the lash myself — my back is scarred with it. I know what they suffer, and I implore you to bring the weight of that powerful public opinion which you can make so effective to bear on the hearts and consciences of the slaveholders of my country. Tell them they must give up their vile practices or continue to be held in contempt by the whole civilized world.' The Hutchinson Family then brought proceedings to a close with a haunting song about a slave mother torn from her daughter at an auction block. Before the crowd dispersed, Haughton apprised them of Douglass's plan to speak in Wexford, Waterford, Cork and other cities in southern Ireland, urging the residents of those cities to 'prepare a hearty reception' for him.

To fill a venue as large as the Music Hall

for three nights, Douglass had clearly broken out of the Quaker, anti-slavery, anti-everythingarian audience to reach a broader spectrum of the people. Many workingmen, indeed, had given up their own time to help set up the hall on the nights of his lectures. They had been moved by Douglass's eloquent testimony of the sufferings of slavery. But they had also come for excitement, accounts of flogging being a sought-after form of nineteenth-century voyeurism, akin to today's tabloid sensationalism. Despite their staid credentials, the Hibernian Anti-Slavery Society had not been shy about pushing this element of the speeches. 'The public streets are placarded with statements, setting forth that Mr Douglass has been a 'slave,' has *bona fide* felt the lash, &c.' wrote Thomas D'Arcy McGee in his 'Letter from Ireland' to the *Boston Pilot*. McGee, one of the 'Young Ireland' group in Daniel O'Connell's Repeal movement, had lived in America for a number of years and was far from enthusiastic about slave emancipation. He was certainly much more circumspect than O'Connell, the great Irish leader with whom a delighted Douglass would share a stage in Dublin.

5

'There Goes Dan, There Goes Dan'

'The first sight I caught of him, after landing in Ireland, was near Sackville Street Bridge,' wrote Frederick Douglass of Daniel O'Connell. 'He was just [up] from Derrynane, his country seat, where he had been spending several months resting from his arduous labours in the cause of Irish liberty.' O'Connell was on his way to give a speech at Conciliation Hall, the recently built headquarters of the Repeal Association, the political organisation he had founded in the spring of 1840. Wrapped up in a long, dark cloak to keep the late September chill at bay, O'Connell walked at a 'rapid rate' towards the great hall. 'There goes Dan! There goes Dan!' shouted a 'squad of ragged little boys' following behind. 'The great man beamed upon the ragged urchins with a look of over-flowing affection and delight, as though they were his own children greeting his coming to his home after a long absence,' Douglass recalled. 'A more beautiful and touching picture it has seldom been my good fortune to witness.'

O'Connell, a lawyer and landowner from

County Kerry, was one of the great political figures of the era, a tall, broad-chested folk hero who in the late 1820s had waged and won the battle for Catholic emancipation in Ireland. This immense success — enabling Irish Catholics to sit in parliament and hold senior offices of state, rights long denied them by the repressive Penal Laws — had earned him the title 'The Liberator'. O'Connell's latest (and last) political crusade was for the repeal of the Act of Union that had placed Ireland under the control of Westminster. Well known for his rejection of violence in the pursuit of political objectives, the Repeal movement was a mirror of the earlier emancipation campaign in its focus on 'people power' and 'moral force', the early years of the decade witnessing a series of huge political gatherings across the country, 'monster meetings' where an ageing but still remarkably robust O'Connell demanded self-government for Ireland.

The high point of the Repeal agitation came in the summer of 1843, when crowds up to half a million strong travelled by foot, horse or carriage to see the revered Liberator at outdoor meetings in places like Cork, Mallow and the Hill of Tara. It was an astonishing show of strength, O'Connell once again seeming to hold the fate of the country in his hands. In October, an alarmed British Prime Minister, Sir Robert Peel, finally responded, banning a meeting in Clontarf the night before it was due to be held. A large number of soldiers with heavy artillery moved to the site of the planned meeting, ready to fire if crowds gathered. Three gunships were also moved into position, with further reinforcements sent to Dublin in case of violence there. Fearing the 'slaughter of the people', O'Connell backed down and cancelled the meeting. He was arrested days later and spent several months in prison in 1844 after being convicted of sedition. O'Connell's release in September saw great celebrations, a massive triumphal carriage, drawn by six white horses, arriving at the prison door to take him through the crowded streets. 'I remember the glory of his triumphant procession out of prison, a harper playing before him' wrote Alfred Webb, just a child at the time. Nevertheless, the spell in prison had made a deep impact, with O'Connell emerging much more cautious politically. The Liberator was also frailer, looking very much his seventy years by the time Douglass saw him cross the bridge that now bears his name. He remained, however, a compelling speaker.

Eager to hear the fabled orator, Douglass

followed O'Connell into Conciliation Hall, the walls of which were decorated with pictures of Irish wolfhounds, round towers and other symbols of Gaelic iconography. He had a letter of introduction from James Haughton but did not need it, the mass of bodies opening up to allow the visitor closer to the front. With twelve large bronze candelabra lighting proceedings, O'Connell looked down upon the crowded hall from a raised platform. He stood magisterially, speaking for over an hour, the journalists packed together near the stage transcribing quickly his powerful words. The 'Repeal flame', he declared, was not 'going out', whatever the claims made in Britain. His proof: a recent meeting in Tipperary, which tens of thousands, perhaps more, had attended. It was, he said, a 'transcendently beautiful spectacle', one of the 'noblest sights that ever Ireland exhibited'.

'How often have the English press taunted us, by saying we had not wisdom, or caution, or prudence enough to govern ourselves,' O'Connell continued.

How often have they said that the Repeal of the Union would only tend to the raising of factions amongst ourselves . . . I ask those who tell us that the people of

Ireland are unfit to govern themselves, what spirit governed them in Tipperary . . . I will tell them — their own judgement and reason . . . and I feel gratified at the idea, that there is not a people in Europe — Ireland alone excepted — where such multitudes could meet and separate without the least violence or ill-will, or tumult of any kind . . . I can look to this demonstration as a proof of the unquestionable fitness of the Irish people for self-government, and self-government they shall have.

Douglass was transfixed.

With all the rest of the world I had heard much of Daniel O'Connell as an orator and as the great man of his country . . . I had heard . . . how he could sway and control the feelings of his people; how he could move them to mirth or tears; how he could rouse to fiercest indignation and wrath; how he could in the open air hold the attention of twenty and even thirty thousand people; still I made allowance for enthusiasm and exaggeration and tempered my thought accordingly; but a few sentences of this man's deep, rich, musical and almost miraculous voice, as it swept over the vast multitude, uttered without effort, without gestures, with arms folded upon his deep, broad chest, dispelled all doubt of the vastness and grandeur of his power with his people, and indeed, with any people who might come under the spell of his eloquence.

The meeting was made all the more memorable for Douglass by the fact that O'Connell — who had no idea of the escaped slave's presence — devoted a large portion of his speech to 'the plague spot of slavery' in America. 'I have been assailed for attacking the American institution, as it is called, Negro slavery,' he told his followers, referring to a recent article in the American journal the *Brownson Review*. 'I am not ashamed of that attack — I do not shrink from it. I am the advocate of civil and religious liberty all over the globe, and wherever tyranny exists I am the foe of the tyrant; wherever oppression shows itself I am the foe of the oppressor — wherever slavery rears its head I am the enemy of the system, or the institution, call it by what name you will.'

'I am the friend of liberty in every clime, class and colour,' O'Connell continued, in words Douglass would be able to quote decades later, 'my sympathy with distress is not confined within the narrow bounds of my own green island — no, it extends itself to every corner of the earth — my heart walks abroad, and wherever the miserable is to be succoured and the slave to be set free, there my spirit is at home, and I delight to dwell in its abode.'

Douglass was inspired, describing O'Connell as a 'broad-hearted philanthropist'. It was an example he would soon seek to emulate.

'Agitate! Agitate! Agitate!'
'Mr O'Connell's method of receiving Americans, visiting his country, was rough on slaveholders,' Douglass recalled approvingly. 'A gentleman from this country being introduced to the Liberator, and about to extend his hand, was suddenly stopped, as O'Connell withdrew his hand, saying: 'Pardon me, sir; but I make it a rule never to give my hand to an American without asking if he is a slaveholder.' The gentleman answered good-naturedly: 'No, Mr O'Connell, I am not a slaveholder, but I am willing to discuss the question of slavery with you.' 'Pardon me again,' said O'Connell. 'Discuss it with me! Without meaning you the least harm in the world, should a gentleman come into my study and propose to discuss with me the rightfulness of picking pockets, I

would show him the door, lest he should be tempted to put his theory into practice.''

O'Connell had been sympathetic to the anti-slavery cause all his life, although it was not until after the passage of Catholic emancipation in 1829 that he really began to campaign for it strongly. 'I am an abolition-ist,' he declared before a meeting in London demanding the end of slavery in the West Indies in the early 1830s. 'I am for speedy, immediate abolition . . . I enter into no compromise with slavery.' O'Connell also attacked slavery in the United States, insisting he would never 'pollute' his feet by 'treading on its shores' while slavery existed. 'America, it is a foul stain upon your character!' he told an audience in Cork, comparing the anti-slavery policies of the South American revolutionary Simón Bolívar with the slave-owning Founding Father George Washington. O'Connell's rhetoric could be incendiary and aggressive, attacking the hypocrisy in the Declaration of Independence and labelling an American Ambassador to London as a slave breeder. But he never forgot the human face of slavery, moving audiences to tears with evocative descriptions of the slave mother, who 'looks upon the child she has borne, and knows that she is but rearing the slave of another . . . Instead of a blessing, she feels that in each child she has been visited with a curse.' Echoing the famous call from his Catholic emancipation campaign, he also repeatedly urged 'some black O'Connell' to rise among the slaves and cry 'Agitate! Agitate! Agitate!'

O'Connell became one of the leading anti-slavery campaigners in the world, forging friendships with American abolitionists like William Lloyd Garrison and celebrated in verse by the American Quaker poet John Greenleaf Whittier. Unsurprisingly, given their combative natures and the size of their egos, the friendship between O'Connell and Garrison did not always run smoothly. Nevertheless, they spent a good deal of time together at the World Anti-Slavery Convention in London in the summer of 1840, where O'Connell delivered one of the keynote addresses, condemning once again American hypocrisy over slavery. As one of the few Catholics to attend the Convention (Richard Robert Madden, the Irish doctor whose testimony helped free the slaves at the famous *Amistad* trial in 1840, was another), he also referred to Pope Gregory XVI's recent Apostolic Letter condemning slavery and the slave trade — in part to demonstrate to the Protestant evangelicals they did not enjoy a monopoly on anti-slavery sentiment. He was

119

received, Garrison wrote in *The Liberator*, 'with a storm of applause that almost shook the building to its foundations'. Douglass's friend Charles Lenox Remond was also in attendance, describing how O'Connell's 'soul-stirring eloquence' and 'burning sarcasm' made 'every fibre of my heart contract'.

A year later, O'Connell's was the most prominent name on the 'Address of the People of Ireland to their Countrymen and Countrywomen in America', the anti-slavery letter calling on Irish Americans to support the abolitionists. Although primarily the work of Richard D. Webb, Richard Allen and Haughton, members of the Repeal Association had joined the Hibernian Anti-Slavery Society in taking the address from door to door around Ireland. They had also collected signatures where the Protestant members of the Hibernian Anti-Slavery Society dared not go — outside Catholic churches on Sunday mornings. More than 60,000 names were collected; an impressive figure, even if many of the signatories were not fully aware of the contents of the address, happy simply to put their name to anything backed by O'Connell. This was not the first time O'Connell and the Hibernian Anti-Slavery Society worked together. In the winter of 1840–41, they had combined in opposition to a scheme for large-scale Irish emigration to the West Indies, which both parties viewed as an attempt to replace the newly freed slaves with white Irish slaves.

O'Connell got on reasonably well with Haughton, a paid-up member of the Repeal Association. Webb, however, was much more ambivalent toward the Liberator. He would, in fact, frown on the manner in which Douglass came to idolise him. 'I would be sorry to see him suffer or crestfallen,' Webb wrote to the American abolitionist Edmund Quincy of O'Connell, calling him at the same time a 'double-tongued pleader' and an 'unscrupulous liar'. Quite unfairly, Webb suspected O'Connell of using the anti-slavery movement simply to enhance his reputation as a great humanitarian. Webb also opposed O'Connell's Repeal campaign, fearing it would lead to the 'ascendancy of the most intolerant of sects' and the 'most bigoted, priest-ridden form of Christianity'. Philanthropic Quakers, it seems, were just as wary as other Protestants of a Catholic-dominated Ireland.

Confident that O'Connell's imprimatur would bring more Irish Americans into their fold, the abolitionists had been delighted with the Irish Address. 'Nine tenths of the Irish are at heart thoroughgoing abolitionists,' John A.

Collins declared hopefully. The abolitionists, however, were soon disappointed, the grand majority of Irish Americans, especially the most recent arrivals, recoiling from any association with radicals like Garrison and his denunciations of the Constitution as they strove for acceptance in mainstream America. John Hughes, the Irish-born Bishop of New York, actually believed O'Connell's signature had been forged at first. (Hughes had previously been dismissive of the Papal address, insisting it related to the slave trade alone, and not slavery in America.) Many newspapers followed suit, denouncing the address as either a fraud or an intolerable interference in American affairs. The *Boston Pilot*, the leading Irish American paper, praised the Irish in America for rejecting the address, thereby proving their loyalty to their adopted country.

'I do not wonder that you blush, and hang your head, to see the unkind and insolent reception which the Irish Address has met with, on this side of the Atlantic, at the hands of your exiled countrymen,' a disappointed Garrison wrote to Allen a few months after the hope-filled launch of the Address at Faneuil Hall. 'It is now quite apparent that they will go *en masse* with southern men-stealers, and in opposition to the anti-slavery movement.' Garrison blamed 'crafty' priests, 'unprincipled political demagogues' and Irish American newspaper editors for poisoning the minds of Irish immigrants against the abolitionists. 'So much more potent is the influence of American slavery over their minds,' he lamented, 'than that of Fr Mathew and Daniel O'Connell combined.'

American Repealers, too, had made clear their displeasure, with societies in Louisiana, Baltimore and Albany publicly condemning the address.

'The American Eagle'

The first meeting of the Loyal National Repeal Association, to give the organisation its full title, was held in Dublin on 15 April 1840, with local branches soon set up across the country. O'Connell's stature among the Irish in America ensured Repeal groups were quickly established there, too, the first by some labourers and tradesmen in Boston in October 1840 — O'Connell had received similar support during his Catholic emancipation campaign. It was not long before thousands of dollars in so-called 'Repeal rent' were making their way across the Atlantic. First to arrive was a cheque for £200 sent from the Philadelphia Repeal society, along with a list of the 900 supporters who had contributed. By October 1841, membership of the Philadelphia group surpassed 3,000.

Although focused on cities with significant Irish populations like Boston, Philadelphia and New York, Repeal groups were also found in small towns and rural areas in more than a dozen states and territories, both North and South. O'Connell, in fact, was soon fending off complaints from abolitionists in Ireland and America about accepting money from the pro-slavery Repeal groups in the South. At first, O'Connell had been happy to accept contributions from the Southern states, as he had during the Catholic emancipation campaign. He said he had no right to deprive Ireland of aid because of his anti-slavery principles, suggesting the best way of proceeding was to convince them in a conciliatory manner of the evil of slavery. He became uneasy, however, and decided to reject all contributions from supporters of slavery. 'We do not want bloodstained money,' he told a meeting of the Repeal Association in Dublin in May 1843. It was a grand, humanitarian gesture, one that was still earning him plaudits from abolitionists in America decades after his death. In truth, however, O'Connell appears to have returned money only once: £178 14s 9d to the New

Orleans Repeal society, the cause some 'physical force' resolutions accompanying the contribution rather than anything to do with slavery.

While the growth of the Repeal movement in America was impressive, O'Connell's efforts to link it with abolition misfired badly. The first National Repeal Convention, held in Philadelphia in February 1842, less than a month after the launch of the Irish Address, warned O'Connell that he would lose support in the United States if he continued to champion abolitionism. A year later, the same body refused to discuss slavery as it was too controversial and exposed Irish immigrants to accusations of being disloyal citizens. Given the heightened state of anti-Catholic, anti-immigrant feeling in America at the time, this would have seemed a valid point to many Irish Americans, tensions between Protestant nativists and Catholic immigrants reaching their apogee in the Philadelphia riots of 1844. The fear that freed slaves would bring greater competition to an already crowded workplace was another not inconsequential factor in the animosity Irish Americans felt towards abolitionists, as was the fact that the two big bodies of which Irish immigrants were most likely to be members — the Democratic Party and the Catholic Church — were either actively or tacitly pro-slavery.

Stung by the negative response to the Irish Address, and with a number of Repealers at home, most notably Young Irelanders like Thomas Davis, Charles Gavan Duffy and John Mitchel, voicing concerns about his anti-slavery statements distracting from the movement's main aim, O'Connell began to distance himself from abolitionists like Garrison. Nevertheless, he continued to speak out against slavery, even as he prepared for 'monster meetings' during the so-called 'Repeal Year' of 1843. 'We will recognise you as Irishmen no longer,' he threatened American Repealers in May, if they continued to justify slavery. A few months later, a letter from Repealers in Cincinnati containing the unsavoury claim that 'the very odour of the Negro is almost insufferable to the white' elicited another scorching rebuke, written just days after the trauma of the cancelled meeting at Clontarf.

O'Connell's persistent attacks on slavery were a source of deep discomfort for Repealers in America, who sought to cover themselves from accusations of disloyalty with declarations of dual patriotism. 'Affection for the green fields of his youth,' one Repeal circular explained, 'will never weaken a man's attachment for the country of his adoption. Affection for the one, is a sure pledge of his fidelity to the other; a pledge never unredeemed by Irishmen.' The Repealers also sought to elect prominent Americans, including Robert Tyler, the son of President John Tyler, to high positions in their societies, hoping to portray themselves as an 'American' and not just an 'Irish American' movement. These tactics would prove wholly insufficient in the face of O'Connell's most notorious anti-slavery address, when he raised the prospect of Ireland lining up with the ancient enemy — Britain — against America in time of war.

'Let not America imagine that this boasting of liberty makes her name respected,' O'Connell began in typical fashion, speaking before a Repeal Association meeting in March 1845. 'No, for as the assertion of virtue is a proof of hypocrisy, if the virtue be not practice, so the attempt to proclaim liberty becomes blasphemous when we see three millions of human beings . . . torn by the lash . . . Shame upon them, and eternal disgrace to them who speak of liberty and practise slavery.' Angered by the recent American annexation of the slave territory of Texas, he went on to declare provocatively that if Repeal was granted, Ireland would support Britain in the then apparently imminent war with America over the jointly controlled Oregon Territory in the Pacific Northwest. 'The throne of Victoria can be made perfectly secure — the honour of the British Empire maintained — and the American eagle in its highest point of flight, be brought down. Let them but give us the parliament in College Green, and Oregon shall be theirs, and Texas shall be harmless.'

Coming at a time of extreme Anglo-American tensions, this incendiary speech — reprinted widely in the American press — placed Irish American Repealers in an invidious position. Would they be a fifth column for Britain in the event of war? In response, Repeal societies across America expressed shock at O'Connell's aggressive language and pledged their allegiance to the 'American eagle'. The Liberator had crossed a line, moving beyond an attack on slavery to an attack on the country itself. O'Connell's 'denunciations against slavery might be tolerated', wrote a correspondent to the *Boston Pilot*, 'but never let him touch a feather in our eagle of liberty under whose fostering wing so many of his fellow-countrymen have found shelter and protection'. A number of Repeal groups in the South disbanded while many in the North were fatally weakened by dissension and the loss of large numbers of members.

And so it was that the Repeal movement in America was disintegrating even as Douglass was pushed by James Buffum to the front of the meeting in Dublin, and up onto the stage with O'Connell.

'The Smallest Relic'

With what has been called the 'affable arrogance' that was characteristic of him, O'Connell introduced Douglass to the large crowd as 'the black O'Connell of the United States'. Coming to the front of the stage, Douglass made a short speech, describing to loud cheers how he had heard O'Connell's name in the 'curses of his masters' years earlier and immediately loved him. He also assured the audience that O'Connell's denunciations of slavery were having a 'great effect' among Americans, before concluding evocatively: 'For, while with one arm the Liberator was bursting the fetters of Irishmen, with the other he was striking off the literal chains from the limbs of the Negro.'

Listening to the fabled orator, standing beside him, hearing the deafening roars of the crowded hall, the Repeal movement must have seemed in good stead to Douglass. The truth, however, was that it was already on the wane, in Ireland as much as America, having never really recovered from the twin disasters of Clontarf and O'Connell's imprisonment. It was also increasingly beset by splits and factionalism, the Young Irelanders, a group of gifted writers clustered around *The Nation*, demanding firmer action from O'Connell. Yearning, in Webb's words, for their own 'Marathon or Thermopylae', the Young Irelanders would go on to lead a rebellion in 1848, many escaping to America in the aftermath of its failure. O'Connell had died by this time, having continued to deteriorate physically.

With the Repeal agitation falling away, an ailing and increasingly devout O'Connell was told by doctors in early 1847 to recuperate in a warmer climate. He seized on this advice as an opportunity to make a pilgrimage to Rome. This was a daunting journey for a man of O'Connell's infirmity and age. He travelled, therefore, in slow, easy stages, sailing from Folkestone in England to Boulogne in France on 22 March and not reaching Italy until early May. O'Connell stopped eating in Genoa — still a distance from Rome — and became delirious, shouting out at his old adversary Sir Robert Peel. He was given the Last Rites by the leading clergy of the city and died on the evening of Saturday 15 May 1847.

The Liberator's body did not arrive back in Ireland until early August, the mourners kneeling down as one on the cold stone ground of Dublin harbour as his huge, red velvet-covered coffin was brought ashore. The black cloth from the temporary chapel on board the *Duchess of Kent* was 'torn up in small fragments' and distributed among the thousands of onlookers seeking 'the smallest relic connected with the remains of the revered Liberator'. O'Connell lay in state for three days before burial in Glasnevin Cemetery in Dublin. 'With my mother we viewed the funeral from Uncle James's shop in Corn Market, and we often visited his grave in the old circle at Glasnevin,' wrote Alfred Webb. 'In later years I saw the house where he died in Genoa, and the spot where his heart is entombed in Rome.'

'No public man was perhaps more beloved by any people than Daniel O'Connell was by the people of his country,' wrote Douglass in 1886, thinking back over his time in Ireland. O'Connell's standing in the anti-slavery movement was also secure, as shown by the appearance of Garrison and other leading abolitionists at a celebratory meeting in Boston held to mark the centenary of the Liberator's birth in August 1875.

Douglass would always speak well of O'Connell; the same was not true of the other major Irish figure with whom he would spend time: Fr Theobald Mathew.

6

'The Apostle of Temperance'

'You know one of my objects in coming here was to get a little repose, that I might return home refreshed and strengthened, ready and able to join you vigorously in the prosecution of our holy cause,' Frederick Douglass reminded William Lloyd Garrison in a letter from Dublin. 'But, really, if the labor of the last two weeks be a fair sample of what awaits me, I have certainly sought repose in the wrong place. I have work enough here, on the spot, to occupy every inch of my time, and every particle of my strength, were I to stay in this city a whole six months . . . I have invitation after invitation to address temperance meetings, which I am compelled to decline. How different here, from my treatment at home! In this country, I am welcomed to the temperance platform, side by side with white speakers, and am received as kindly and warmly as though my skin were white.'

Although wary of distracting from the anti-slavery cause by speaking publicly on other subjects, Douglass made an exception for temperance, the two movements long synonymous with each other on both sides of the Atlantic. In America, there was a sense that temperance was essential to black elevation. 'Wherever it can be said that the free blacks are a sober, industrious and intelligent people, capable of self-government, the only argument in favour of slavery falls to the ground,' wrote the black newspaper owner Stephen Meyers, a contemporary of Douglass's whose home in Albany now forms part of the New York State Underground Railway Heritage Trail. Northern free blacks had in fact been among the first to form temperance groups in the country in the early nineteenth century. In the South, meanwhile, as Douglass knew only too well, masters dulled the spirits of their slaves by plying them with alcohol on Sundays or holidays like Christmas. 'I have known slaveholders resort to cunning tricks, with a view of getting their slaves deplorably drunk,' he wrote. 'A usual plan is, to make bets on a slave, that he can drink more whiskey than any other; and so to induce a rivalry among them, for the mastery in this degradation. The scenes, brought about in this way, were often scandalous and loathsome in the extreme. Whole multitudes might be found stretched out in brutal drunkenness, at once helpless and disgusting.'

'I knew once what it was to drink with all the ardour of an *old soaker*,' Douglass admitted, recalling his time as a lowly field-hand on the Eastern Shore. 'I lived with a Mr Freeland who used to give his slaves apple brandy. Some of the slaves were not able to drink their own share, but I was able to drink my own and theirs too. I took it because it made me feel I was a great man. I used to think I was a president.' It was not long, however, before Douglass saw through the apparent kindness for what it really was: another way to keep the minds of slaves away from thoughts of freedom. He began to view temperance as an important step on the path to slave emancipation, his first public appearance in Ireland actually coming at a temperance rally rather than an anti-slavery meeting, taken to Celbridge in County Kildare by James Haughton and James H. Webb the day he landed in Dublin.

They travelled by carriage, making their way slowly through the crowded roads leading into the village, local temperance bands playing music as the vast assemblage converged in a nearby field owned by a farmer named Cooney. Haughton and a few others made speeches, Douglass himself saying a few words and being warmly applauded. Fr John Spratt, a Carmelite friar, then moved through the

134

5,000-strong crowd, administering the total abstinence pledge. It was a remarkable scene, replicated many times in a country where it was estimated more than 5 million people had taken the pledge.

Newspaper reports emphasised the cheerfulness of the occasion and the presence of magistrates, 'elegantly attired' ladies and members of the local landed gentry encouraging their tenants and workmen to join the cause. Douglass, however, was struck by how closely the poorest Irish country people resembled his enslaved brethren across the Atlantic.

> Never did human faces tell a sadder tale. More than five thousand were assembled; and I say, with no wish to wound the feelings of any Irishman, that these people lacked only a black skin and woolly hair, to complete their likeness to the plantation negro. The open, uneducated mouth — the long, gaunt arm — the badly formed foot and ankle — the shuffling gait — the retreating forehead and vacant expression . . . all reminded me of the plantation, and my own cruelly abused people.

Fr Spratt, the main speaker in Celbridge, had been one of the founders of the temperance movement in Ireland in the 1830s. The real leader, however, was the Cork-based Franciscan priest Fr Theobald Mathew, the so-called 'Apostle of Temperance'.

Mathew's 'Miracle'

The first concerted temperance movement began in America in the early nineteenth century, led for the most part by evangelical Protestant ministers. Its influence spread across the Atlantic, the first temperance societies in Ireland established in Belfast, Dublin and New Ross in 1829, Richard D. Webb among the founders of the Dublin group. (He would publish a great deal of temperance literature and compose his own anti-drink ballads.) Although Protestants were again to the fore, a number of Catholic priests also got involved, including the aforementioned Fr Spratt. Initially, the temperance societies in Ireland were anti-spirits rather than anti-drink. It was not long, however, before more militant teetotallers took over the movement, total abstinence seeming to offer a clearer solution to the country's deeply embedded problems with drink. The campaign had some success. Nevertheless, it was not until Fr Mathew joined the movement that it really broke through to the Catholic masses.

With three Catholic archbishops among his

forebears, it is no surprise that the Tipperary-born Mathew found himself drawn to a life of religion, joining the Capuchins at their Church Street Friary in Dublin in 1808. Of Italian provenance and following the teachings of St Francis, the Capuchins in Ireland were small in number and at something of a remove from the main Catholic clergy. Ordained a priest in 1813, Mathew was assigned to the Blackamoor Lane Friary in Cork city. He dedicated the next two decades of his life to helping the sick and poor of the city and surrounding countryside. He even learned Irish, still the main language of many of the poorest country people. A gentle and well-respected figure around the city, he set up schools and became involved in various local bodies, including the Cork House of Industry, a non-sectarian home for the sick and elderly poor, where the Quaker reformer William 'Billy' Martin was a fellow director. Martin, later one of the Irish delegates to the World Anti-Slavery Convention in London, had set up the Cork Total Abstinence Society in the mid-1830s. Recognising the need for a Catholic figurehead to grow the movement, he convinced his friend Mathew to join the cause in 1838.

Prior to joining the Cork Total Abstinence Society, Mathew had often enjoyed a glass of whiskey or wine. Two of his brothers owned distilleries, and during the cholera epidemic of 1832, he sent bottles of whiskey to the hospitals for the treatment of the sick. (He was not the only one: five local doctors felt compelled to write a letter to the mayor warning against the common belief that whiskey was 'the best preventative' against the disease.) Nevertheless, once convinced of the cause, the by now 47-year-old Mathew spent almost every hour of the day advocating temperance and administering the pledge. He transformed the Cork Total Abstinence Society into the largest temperance organisation in the British Isles, its membership growing from about 2,000 to over 20,000 in his first year as president. National papers took note and he started to gain some celebrity, with people coming from all Munster and beyond to receive the pledge at his hands, often knocking on his door in the middle of the night. Travelling long distances gave the undertaking the feel of a pilgrimage, which was attractive to the Catholic Irish psyche. The people also felt the pledge carried more weight if taken from Mathew than a local priest. Many, in fact, started to believe he could cure their illnesses.

Although never a great speaker, Mathew's compassionate manner drew people to him.

Like Daniel O'Connell and Abraham Lincoln, two other great figures from the age, he had a fount of simple anecdotes and stories to which ordinary people could relate. There was also a real sense of occasion in taking the pledge, the applicant kneeling before Mathew and vowing not to consume any alcohol for any reason for the rest of their lives. Mathew made the sign of the cross above their heads and bestowed his blessing. The new members then received a certificate and had a medal pinned to their chests.

Mathew's success in Cork was soon replicated countrywide, the Apostle of Temperance travelling relentlessly through all four provinces administering the pledge. To give just two examples of the vast crowds he attracted, he pledged more than 100,000 people over the course of two days in Limerick in November 1839 and another 85,000 in Birr, County Offaly, the following March. Elsewhere, almost the entire populations of some towns and villages took the pledge. The fact that many quickly fell back into old drinking habits in no way diminishes the dramatic impact of the movement: the number of gallons of spirits consumed in Ireland fell by almost 50 per cent between 1838 and 1844. A large number of distilleries (including one owned by one of his brothers), public houses and whiskey retailers also shut down, while convictions for serious crime decreased by about 33 per cent from 12,049 to 8,042. Temperance, described by O'Connell as a 'moral and majestic miracle', was not the only factor in this decline in crime, but it was a significant one.

By 1843 more than half the population of Ireland had taken the pledge, and Mathew became the only rival to O'Connell for the affections of the country. His crusade had turned into a mass movement, teetotalism insinuating itself into the fabric of Irish society, with temperance bands playing music at public events, temperance groups taking the lead in St Patrick's Day parades and newspapers full of notices for books with titles like *The Evils of Intemperance*. The jobs pages, too, bore the imprint of the temperance movement: 'Wanted — A Steady Active Man — To take the entire charge of my horses . . . No person need apply who cannot keep himself perfectly Sober.' Those seeking employment also made sure to mention they had taken the pledge: 'To Wine Merchants, Grocers etc — Wants a Situation as Porter, a smart, active young man, who is a teetotaller for the last three years, and perfectly understands bottling, pickling etc.'

Touring Ireland in 1842, the English novelist and satirist William Makepeace Thackeray heard complaints that Mathew had taken 'all the fun' out of the country. Thackeray saw him in Cork, the Apostle of Temperance having a cup of tea in the Imperial Hotel on the South Mall as the author and some friends struggled in for breakfast and a soda-water cure after a night's drinking. 'Some of us felt a little ashamed of ourselves and did not like to ask somehow for the soda-water in such an awful presence as that. Besides, it would have been a confession to a Catholic priest and, as a Protestant, I am above that.' Despite these barbs, Thackeray was impressed with Mathew, who had got into trouble with the Church hierarchy over his willingness to work with Protestants and members of other religious faiths, like Webb, Allen and Haughton.

'There is nothing remarkable in Fr Mathew's manner, except that it is exceedingly simple, hearty and manly and that he does not wear the downcast . . . look which, I know not why, characterises the chief part of the gentlemen of his profession,' Thackeray wrote.

Whence comes that general scowl which darkens the faces of the Irish priesthood? I have met a score of these reverend

141

gentlemen in the country and not one of them seemed to look or speak frankly, except Fr Mathew and a couple more. He is almost the only man, too, that I have met in Ireland, who, in speaking of public matters, did not talk as a partisan . . . And it was impossible in hearing him to know . . . whether he was a Whig or Tory, Catholic or Protestant. Why does not Government make a Privy Councillor of him? — that is, if he would honour the Right Honourable body by taking a seat amongst them.

His knowledge of the people is prodigious and their confidence in him as great and what a touching attachment that is which these poor fellows show to anyone who has their cause at heart.

Thackeray continued: 'He never misses a chance of making a convert and has his hand ready and a pledge in his pocket for sick or poor.' When a waiter, one of his 'disciples', came into the room, Mathew 'recognised him and shook him by the hand directly; as he did with the strangers who were presented to him and not with a courtly popularity-hunting air, but, as it seemed, from sheer hearty kindness and a desire to do everyone good.'

Douglass had heard of Fr Mathew in

America. In Dublin, he saw him from afar, administering the pledge to about 1,000 people in the village of Booterstown. He finally met the Apostle of Temperance more than a month later, at a soirée held in the escaped slave's honour in Cork.

'All Great Reforms Go Together'

With more than 250 of the city's 'most respectable' citizens in attendance, the South Main Street Quadrille Band playing in the gallery and an abundance of tea, fruit and confectionary being served, Mathew introduced Douglass onto the stage of the Cork Temperance Institute on Academy Street.

'Intemperance stalks abroad among the coloured people of my country,' Douglass told the gathering, regretting how the drunken behaviour of free blacks in the North held back the anti-slavery movement. 'They have furnished arguments to the oppressors for oppressing us.' Some progress had been made, he said, citing the example of Philadelphia, where the number of free black temperance groups had more than doubled in recent years. But even here there were difficulties: a parade of black temperance societies in the city had been attacked by a white mob, who tore up banners, beat up marchers and set fire to a local black church. Douglass ended on a positive note, giving voice to his increasingly strong sense that reformers, no matter what their country or cause, were linked as one. 'All great reforms go together,' he declared. 'Whatever tends to elevate, whatever tends to exalt humanity in one portion of the world, tends to exalt it in another part; the same feeling that warms the heart of the philanthropist here, animates that of the lover of humanity in every country.'

Describing the night to Garrison, Douglass was struck once again by the openness of the audience to a person of his colour. 'Amongst them all, I saw no one that seemed to be shocked or disturbed at my dark presence. No one seemed to feel himself contaminated by contact with me. I think it would be difficult to get the same number of persons together in any of our New England cities, without some democratic nose growing deformed at my approach. *But then you know white people in America are whiter, purer and better than the people here. This accounts for it!*' The following morning, Douglass enjoyed a memorable breakfast with Mathew. 'Welcome! Welcome, my dear Sir, to my humble abode,' Mathew called, rushing out to greet Douglass 30 yards from his house. It was a simple, unprepossessing home, Mathew guiding Douglass by the hand through a 'rough' passage and up some stairs to the main room. There was no carpet on the floor and very little furniture, just an old-fashioned sideboard, a table and chairs and three or four pictures hung 'carelessly' around the walls. 'The breakfast table was set when I went in,' Douglass recalled. 'A large urn stood in the middle, surrounded by cups, saucers, plates, knives and forks . . . all of a very plain order . . . too plain, I thought, for so great a man.'

William O'Connor, a wealthy landowner who had erected a medieval-style round tower — instantly dubbed the 'Tower of Temperance' — on the outskirts of the city to celebrate and commemorate Mathew's tour of England in 1843, was also present. Although an admirer of Mathew's, O'Connor challenged him gently on the damage his campaign was doing to the distillers of Cork. Such men, Mathew replied, 'had no right to prosper by the ruin of others'. Douglass seemed quite in awe of Mathew. 'His whole soul appeared to be wrapped up in the temperance cause . . . His time, strength and money are all freely given to the cause; and his success is truly wonderful. When he is at home, his house is literally surrounded with persons, many of whom have come miles to take the pledge. He was called away twice while I was there.' Although teetotal for eight years, Douglass saw the opportunity of taking the pledge from the man he called the 'living saviour of Ireland' as too good to pass up. 'He complied with promptness, and gave me a beautiful silver badge. I now reckon myself with delight the fifth of the last five of Father Mathew's 5,487,495 temperance children.'

Douglass's admiration for Mathew and his work could not disguise the fact that drunkenness was 'still rife in Ireland', with devastating consequences for many. On one of his first days in Dublin, Douglass came upon a beggar with a white cloth wrapped around the upper part of his face. The beggar was feeling his way slowly along a street, a cane in one hand, the other stretched out, soliciting aid. 'His feeble step and singular appearance led me to inquire into his history,' wrote Douglass. The beggar told him he had been a heavy drinker for many years, going on to describe how a 'hog' had bitten off part of his nose while he lay asleep on the road one night in a drunken stupor. 'I looked under the cloth, and saw the horrible spectacle of a living man with face of a skeleton.'

Douglass blamed alcohol almost entirely for Ireland's poverty, a superficial judgement that suggests no matter how fond the escaped slave became of the country, he did not really attain any deep understanding of its social and economic problems. Too much of an Anglophile to allow for the possibility of British policies playing any part in Ireland's troubles, he was also naturally influenced by the company he kept, cocooned for the vast majority of his time in the country in the prosperous Protestant world of which the Quakers were a part. The slow relaxation and eventual ending of the Penal Laws may have seen large numbers of Catholics rise to positions of prominence in business and politics. Nevertheless, there remained a stark divide between the two religions — one Douglass never really crossed, despite sharing stages with Catholic Ireland's two favourite sons.

Douglass would praise O'Connell for the rest of his life. His attitude to Mathew, however, turned sour almost as soon as the famous temperance advocate arrived on a long-planned tour of America in 1849.

'He Too Has Fallen'

Arriving in New York in early July, Mathew was greeted off the boat by the mayor and thousands of cheering Irish men and women. He stayed in the city for three weeks, administering the pledge to more than 20,000 people as he was shepherded around Catholic churches, schools and charities, one of the main aims of his tour being to encourage those immigrants who had taken the pledge in Ireland to remain faithful to it. He travelled to Boston at the end of the month, making an immediate impact. 'Mathew is doing great good here,' wrote Wendell Phillips, the famous orator and lawyer who was second only to Garrison in the abolitionist movement. 'In one street where there were sixteen grog shops his presence has closed all but three. Among the Irish population none but he can effectively reach and they flock to him.' It was also in Boston, however, that Mathew became embroiled in a controversy with Garrison.

A teetotaller for many years, Garrison called to Mathew's rooms at Adams House, the downtown hotel in which he was lodged by supporters. They spoke happily at first, Mathew assuring Garrison that he had 'some very warm friends in Cork'. Remembering Mathew's support for the Irish Address, Garrison invited him to a forthcoming anti-slavery rally in nearby Worcester, hoping an appearance by the Apostle of Temperance would persuade more Irish Americans to join the cause. Mathew, however, determined to avoid such an explosive issue, declined immediately, saying, 'I have as much as I can do to save men from the slavery of intemperance, without attempting the overthrow of any other kind of slavery.' He also seemed to suggest that there was nothing in the Bible prohibiting slavery.

To cries of 'Shame! Shame!' an enraged Garrison recounted Mathew's words to the Worcester rally. A few days later, an abolitionist named Rogers, who had just taken the pledge from Mathew, went to Adams House, returning his pledge together with a protest against the compromise the temperance leader had made with 'women-whippers and baby-stealers'. Garrison next took to the pages of *The Liberator*, denouncing Mathew in a series of open letters. 'In Ireland, you professed to be an uncompromising abolitionist; you found time to bear a strong testimony against American slavery, as a disgrace to the country and a sin against God ... Now that you are on American soil you have signified your determination to give the slave no token of your sympathy, and his oppressor no cause of uneasiness ... You have added to the anguish, horror and despair of the poor miserable slaves, made their yokes heavier, and fastened their chains more securely.'

Where Garrison raged, Douglass mourned. 'Nothing reveals more completely ... the all-prevailing presence . . . of slavery in this land, than the sad fact that scarcely a single foreigner who ventures on our soil, is found able to withstand its pernicious and seductive influence . . . We had fondly hoped, from an acquaintance with Fr Mathew, that his would be a better fate; that he would not change his morality by changing his location . . . We are however grieved, humbled and mortified to know that HE too, has fallen.' Over time, however, Douglass's language grew stronger, the abolitionist condemning Mathew for deserting his 'principles' and sailing instead with the 'popular breeze', reprimanding him for saying that there was nothing in the Bible against slavery, 'thus throwing the whole weight of his religious and philanthropic character on the side of the slaveholders' argument', and describing his efforts to ingratiate himself with a slavery-supporting temperance leader in Georgia as 'servile, cringing, fawning'.

Mathew's stance infuriated anti-slavery activists back home, too. 'I am truly sorry to learn that Fr Mathew has acted a cowardly part on the question of slavery since he arrived in America,' wrote Haughton to an American newspaper. 'I am sorry he has fallen; I am sorry he has bowed down before the slave power.' Webb was even more

150

forthright, telling the American abolitionist Anne Warren Weston that Mathew was 'not worthy to tie Garrison's shoes'. Webb's wife, Hannah, was also hurt and confused by the whole affair. 'I know that Garrison is right & I am wrong & yet I wish to see the man handled more gently,' she wrote, conscious of Mathew's recent stroke and ill health, one of the reasons behind the trip to America, indeed, being to spend the winter months in the warm climate of the South rather than cold, damp Ireland.

Writing to Webb in 1846, Mathew had expressed his 'abhorrence of that detestable system, American slavery'. Nevertheless, the anti-slavery movement had only ever been of minor concern to him — temperance would always come first. In a letter written from Alabama in March 1850, Mathew explained to a friend that his stance in Boston had been necessary, as, had he been prevented from visiting the South because of his support for abolitionism, many Irish people there would have remained 'slaves' to drink. The American correspondent of the *Cork Examiner* — edited by Mathew's friend and future biographer John Francis Maguire — agreed, arguing that if the Apostle of Temperance had attacked slavery, he would have been rendered 'powerless to help his white slaves'.

151

Cork anti-slavery campaigner Isabel Jennings, too, took a softer view. 'Although I feel that I would gladly lay down my life, were it needed, in the anti-slavery cause, yet I also feel that you would injure the temperance cause were you to devote any of your time to the anti-slavery question. One great philanthropic object you have devoted your mind to try and accomplish; and, if you succeed in destroying intemperance in the slave states, you lay the axe at the root of slavery.'

Although Mathew was hurt by the attacks, they did little damage to his tour, which continued at first through New England states like Connecticut and Rhode Island. As autumn turned to winter, Mathew headed south, stopping off in cities like Baltimore, Richmond and Savannah before settling in Charleston and New Orleans for longer periods of time. He had been feted by politicians in Washington and even dined with the slave-owning President Zachery Taylor at the White House. Mathew would stay in America until autumn 1851, criss-crossing the nation and giving the pledge to an estimated half a million people, mostly Irish. Many kept the pledge all their lives, becoming in later years leaders of the Catholic Total Abstinence Union of America. Mathew also boasted that he had come across thousands of people who had taken the pledge from him in Ireland as children and kept it.

The tour, however, was not an unqualified success: his efforts at raising funds to pay off the large debts he had incurred in the then still-uncompleted construction of the Holy Trinity church in Cork and in the provision of so many millions of temperance medals — made by a company in Birmingham and generally distributed by Mathew free of charge — fell far short of expectations. (Despite the size of the movement, Mathew did not have O'Connell's fundraising nous.) The constant speaking, preaching and travelling also did further damage to his health, Mathew suffering a second — near fatal — stroke in Nashville, Tennessee, in March 1851. He would stop touring once back in Ireland, dying on 8 December 1856 at the age of sixty-six. After a large procession through Cork, he was buried at St Joseph's cemetery, the non-sectarian burial ground he had established twenty-six years earlier on the outskirts of the city. 'It is a handsome piece of ground and was formerly a botanic garden,' wrote Thackeray. 'The poor may be buried here for nothing and here, too, once more — thank God! — each may rest without priests or parsons scowling hell-fire at his neighbour unconscious under the grass.'

Prior to leaving Ireland for America in 1849, Mathew had assured a crowd of well-wishers in Cork that the temperance movement was still strong. In truth, however, it had been in decline even before Douglass's arrival in the country. At the soirée held in his honour in Cork, Douglass had tried to laugh away the impression that temperance was struggling: ''Twas going down — going gloriously down — going down east, down west, down north, down to every point of the compass — going into every family — spreading peace and comfort and gladness over the entire community.' There were a number of factors behind the decline, including the rise of the Repeal movement, which diverted people's attention away from temperance, and Mathew's own increasingly distracting financial difficulties.

The decline would become even more precipitous during the Famine, the first signs of which had started to appear as Douglass prepared to leave Dublin and travel down to Wexford.

7

'The Sufferings and Cruelties around Us'

The coach from Dublin to Wexford left Dawson Street every morning at seven o'clock, travelling through towns and villages like Bray, Rathdrum, Arklow, Ferns (where it changed horses) and Enniscorthy. It was a ten-hour journey over roughly surfaced roads, the piles of luggage balanced precariously on top growing higher as more passengers climbed aboard. With the two-horse coach carrying anywhere between twelve and twenty tightly packed passengers at a time, motion sickness was a common complaint. The scenery, however, was quite beautiful en route, rust-red leaves upon the trees, especially around the Glen of the Downs and the Vale of Avoca.

Frederick Douglass, James Buffum and Richard Davis Webb were on their way to stay with Joseph Poole, a young Quaker cousin of Webb's in Wexford. Maria Waring, Webb's sister-in-law, travelled with them. Douglass was a 'fine man', she wrote to a relative soon after the journey, striking a kinder note than the later 'wild animal' statement. 'I wish thee could have heard him speak and the Hutchinsons sing.' The 27-year-old Waring was an impressive, independent-minded young woman and committed anti-slavery campaigner. She had gone to the World Anti-Slavery Convention in London in 1840 and would remain involved in the cause all her life. Nevertheless, as the coach bearing Douglass travelled down the east coast of Ireland, her mind turned to problems closer to home. 'It is unnatural and wrong to pass over the sufferings and cruelties around us for those that are at a distance. The humanity of those who do so is very questionable.'

The propriety of asking an impoverished people to aid strangers several thousands of miles away was an issue Douglass would have to confront over the next few months, especially as the effects of a serious potato blight, the first reports of which had started to emerge while he was in Dublin, became ever clearer, ever graver.

'The Failure of the Potato Crop'
When Douglass first arrived in Ireland, newspapers were reporting happily on the 'abundant supply' of potatoes coming to market. Within a few days, however, an unknown blight had

156

started to damage the crop, reducing the potatoes to a putrid, black mass. Originating on the eastern seaboard of the United States in 1843, *phytophthora infestans*, the fungus that caused the blight, had reached Belgium, France and the Netherlands by the early summer of 1845. Its spread was aided by a developing international trade in seed potatoes, with vessels from any number of American ports, such as New York, Philadelphia and Baltimore, liable to have brought diseased potatoes to Europe. Thriving in the damp, mild conditions that prevailed that summer, it was not long before Irish papers were carrying reports of the appearance of the mysterious disease in parts of England and Scotland. By early September, the blight had arrived in Ireland.

The potential for danger was clear, no other country in Europe as reliant on the potato as Ireland. Indeed, for nine months of the year vast tracts of the Irish population survived on little more than potatoes and some buttermilk or herring, the potatoes boiled in an iron pot or ember-roasted before being eaten communally out of a basket. An adult male would eat up to 14 lb per day; less in June, July and August, the 'hungry months' before harvest. It was a bland, repetitive diet, but it was also quite nutritious. As a crop, it seemed to suit the country perfectly, easy to grow even on bogs and rocky hillsides. It was also an extremely high-yielding crop, important in a country whose population had almost doubled since the turn of the century. By 1845, it was the staple food for more than 3 million of the poorest people in the country.

The initial response to the arrival of the blight in Ireland was quite restrained. The country was used to periodic crop failures and food shortages. (Pigs and other farm animals that were also fed extensively on potatoes generally felt the brunt of these shortages.) It was not until October that the real impact became clear. This was the month in which the Irish dug up most of their potatoes — later than in many other countries. More than half the crop, it was discovered, had been destroyed, the heavy rains facilitating the progress of the disease. 'We deeply regret to say that the accounts reaching us, from all quarters, in regard to the failure of the potato crop are alarming,' wrote the *Wexford Independent*. 'Where potatoes were believed generally if not altogether safe a week or ten days past, it is now found that they are infected, and by entire masses become totally unfit for use.'

The real impact of the shortage would not be felt until the following spring. Nevertheless, the country was clearly on the edge of distress as Douglass made his way into what Webb's son Alfred would recall as the delightful, entrancing, narrow streets of Wexford, where 'from the coach-roof at a few points in the Main Street one could shake hands . . . with people in the windows on both sides' and where 'house after house was occupied by Friends carrying on different businesses and selling behind their own counters'.

'Worse Than Dogs'

Major Robert Cuppage, Captain Thomas Holmes and Francis Randall, three Englishmen who arrived in Ireland as part of Oliver Cromwell's New Model Army in 1649, were (together with their families) the first Quakers to settle in Wexford. Indeed, it was at Randall's home in Edermine near Enniscorthy that the first Quaker meeting in the county took place in 1657. It appears all three men had been 'convinced' — to use the preferred Quaker terminology — while serving as soldiers in the early 1650s, attracted perhaps, after years of bloody fighting, to the mixture of pacifism and spiritual militancy offered by the Friends.

To the chagrin of senior officers and officials, Cuppage, Holmes and Randall were

159

far from the only soldiers to be converted by the Quaker preachers travelling around Ireland at this time. 'Our worst enemy now are the Quakers, who begin to grow in some reputation in the County of Cork, their meetings being attended frequently by Col. Phaier, Major Waller & moste of the chief officers thereabouts,' the Lord Lieutenant Henry Cromwell wrote to the Secretary of State John Thurloe in 1655. 'Some of our souldiers have been perverted by them, & amongst the rest his highness's cornet to his own troop is a professed Q. and hath written to me in their stile . . . I think their principles & practices are not very consistent with civil government, much less the discipline of an army.'

Like Quakers across the country, Cuppage, Holmes and Randall were persecuted for their faith. Randall, for example, was beaten up by soldiers after attending a meeting at the home of another Quaker in New Ross in 1660. The officer in charge told the men to do anything they pleased to the Quakers, they being 'worse than dogs'. Randall was later imprisoned for two years in Wexford jail, for refusing to pay for the christening of his children and for absenting himself from public worship. Holmes, meanwhile, later surveyor general of Pennsylvania, seemed to spend a few days in Newgate jail any time he travelled to Dublin. He was also seized at a meeting in Cashel, County Tipperary, in 1657 and violently thrown out of the town. In time, Holmes would help compile a catalogue of such attacks on Quakers in an epistle entitled *A Narrative of the Cruel Sufferings of the People of God in the Nation of Ireland Called Quakers Addressed to the Parliament of London.*

The native Irish, too, were a threat to the Quakers: a band of six 'lusty young men' raided Cuppage's Lambstown home in March 1665. With 'pistols & their swords drawn, calling him dogge rogue & bad words . . . they tooke away his moneys, plate, lynnen, woollen, ripped open some of the bolsters & bedding, & let the feathers about the roome'. Attacks of this nature, however, had less to do with religion than resentment at the confiscation of Irish lands for use as payment to Cromwell's soldiers. This had certainly been the way in which Cuppage and Holmes came to own their lands in Wexford, Randall, too, most likely.

Despite these trials, the Quaker community grew steadily across Wexford. Meeting Houses were built at Crossabeg, Camolin, Ferns, Taghmon, Enniscorthy and Wexford town. There was certainly a significant Quaker

161

community in the county by the time of the United Irishmen rebellion of 1798. This was one of the bloodiest episodes in Irish history, leaving more than 30,000 people dead. Much of the fighting between the rebel and government forces centred on Wexford, with sectarian outrages committed by both sides. Quaker homes were raided and livestock stolen. No Quaker, however, appears to have been killed. 'They had not taken part in the oppression of the people,' wrote Alfred Webb in later years, the want of casualties a 'singular proof that intolerable wrongs — not religion — were the mainspring of the revolt'.

With the danger of rebellion clear for some years, Quakers around Ireland had been quietly encouraged to destroy any guns they owned for hunting. Joseph Haughton, for example, a relative of James, took his fowling piece to the main street of Ferns and broke it up for all to see. Others dropped their guns rather sadly into the River Moy. When the rebellion came, Quakers nursed and fed anyone they could, irrespective of religion or political attachment. Their lawns and kitchens were filled with fugitive rebels or hungry soldiers. They also helped bury the dead after the Battle of Vinegar Hill, one of the most vicious and pivotal engagements in the failed rebellion.

Richard D. Webb's grandmother was among the Quakers living in Wexford during the rebellion, and his son Alfred would remember being told stories of her cooking meals for the insurgents while they occupied the town, even throwing them out of her kitchen when they became unruly. On one occasion, government troops appeared at the door just as some rebels were sitting down in the kitchen. The rebels fled out the back door, the soldiers coming in to eat the meal in their stead.

Webb's close ties to Wexford made it a natural first stop when he took visiting abolitionists like Douglass out of Dublin.

'The Liberty-Loving Sons of Old Ireland'

On Wednesday 8 October 1845, Douglass appeared before a largely Quaker audience in the bright Georgian meeting room upstairs in the Assembly Rooms in Wexford, for a second night in succession. The *Wexford Independent*, a pro-Repeal newspaper published by John Greene, seven-time mayor of the town, carried an advertisement for the talk, Webb's forward planning clear to see. Douglass would be on stage at eight o'clock in the evening, tickets available at the door for 4d. The notice was found among advertisements for life insurance companies, clothes shops and a recently opened tea shop in the town. Thomas Naylor of Main Street, meanwhile, had 'just received his Winter Supply of Candles, direct from the several manufacturers in England'. Naylor also sold luxury goods, including the 'celebrated' French chocolate made by Adolphe Lafont in Paris, Cork whiskey that was five years in bond, Havana cigars, good lump sugar and coffee. 'Particular care and attention' was given to the selection of this last article, 'combined with the most judicious treatment in its toasting, which is executed on a new and highly improved system under the personal inspection of the Proprietor'.

There do not seem to have been any reporters present at Douglass's talk. A few days later, however, Joseph Poole (a would-be poet and lively letter-writer) sent an account into the papers, his excessively wordy style typical of the time.

Mr Editor — You are without doubt an anti-slavery man, and will have pleasure in informing your readers, who may be unaware of the fact, that the execrable system of American Slavery has had a most complete exposure in our good town of Wexford, at the hands of one of its fugitive victims, and most eloquent and determined opponents, Frederick Douglass, of Lynn, Massachusetts, recently a slave in Maryland, and now threatened in his life and liberty for his courageous denunciation of its iniquity, and who has been driven thereby from the land of stars and stripes — the land of freedom and equality — the land of religion and civilization — the United States of America, to seek protection from the pitiless grip of his master in the bosom of the Green Island, in the hearts and beneath the sheltering arm of the liberty-loving sons of Old Ireland.

This Frederick Douglass — this chattel, this thing, this article of property worth $1,000 at the auction block of the capital of America, proclaimed aloud in the Assembly Room on Wednesday evening his manhood and the manhood of his race and its identity with the whole brotherhood of man. 'I am your brother,' said Douglass, and the assent of his hearers was proclaimed in such an universal shout of approbation that the old walls shook to hear three million of our brothers and sisters still languish in bondage of the most hideous description in the Southern States of America — but the day we doubt not is near when through the instrumentality of such advocates as Douglass, in disseminating a thorough knowledge of the system, and before the contempt and abhorrence of civilized nations, surrounding them like a wall of fire upon all sides, the tyrants of the plantation must at last be shamed or terrified into breaking every yoke and letting the oppressed go free.

Will you through the medium of your paper help forward the good cause by making known the feeling of a large assembly of your fellow townsmen, expressed in the following resolution which passed the meeting without a single dissenting voice.

Proposed by Joseph Poole; seconded by William Whitney:

Resolved — That we have listened with interest to the development of the horrors of American slaveholding in the United States, by Frederick Douglass (recently a slave in that country) and that we are filled with the greatest disgust and loathing at the horrible inconsistency between the profession and practice of those who — calling themselves <u>Christians, Republicans</u> and <u>Democrats</u>, hold men, women and children in the most degrading bondage, and we hereby register our remonstrance against all such, and declare, that as lovers of liberty — as Irishmen having human hearts and human sympathies, we utter our solemn conviction, that no Slaveholder can be Christian any more than <u>Pirates</u> and <u>Robbers</u> can be honest men; and we hereby repudiate all such as the enemies of the human race and the rights of man.

Accounts of such meetings and such resolutions taking place, or being passed in Ireland or England finding their way into the American papers, are well known to be influential in affecting public opinion in America, in disheartening those stealers of men, American Slaveholders, and in strengthening the hands of those devoted friends of the slave and of human freedom the world over, who are now exerting every faculty which God has given them, in their endeavour to wipe out this plague spot from their land.

Douglass also received favourable mention in the *Wexford Conservative*, albeit in the middle of a rambling anti-Catholic diatribe. The anonymous author had been quite taken by a story the light-skinned Douglass told about how two white Americans had chatted to him amiably while travelling by coach through Vermont one night. 'As soon as the light broke in upon them, one of the gentlemen peeped under the hat of Douglass, then suddenly throwing himself back, he stirred his companion and whispered to him, 'By God, it's a nigger!'' The two men were prejudiced against 'the tincture of the poor creole's skin', the author wrote. 'Had they turned their eyes upon their own . . . hearts, they would have seen real blackness in them, not superficially, but throughout all their recesses.'

Like Charles Lenox Remond before them, Douglass and Buffum continued south from Wexford to Waterford, a medium-sized port city that already enjoyed an excellent reputation for glassmaking. They would be hosted by more Pooles, yet another branch of the extended Webb family.

'O, Base America'

Even before Douglass arrived in the city, the *Waterford Mail* had published an editorial extolling the virtues of his *Narrative*.

The author of the present narrative is a man of colour — a fugitive slave — one upon whose flesh the galling lash has imprinted its ruthless fangs, upon whose limbs the gyre and manacle have left their corroding brand, and who now seeks to awaken in the breasts of his fellow Christians, and fellow-men sympathy, for over three million of beings pining in bondage and suffering. The work to which we would now direct attention is well-written, and exposes in all its hideous deformity the accursed system of slavery, whose contaminating influence, like a foul leprosy, taints all it approaches. Mr Douglass has, for the last four years, been travelling as lecturing agent of the American Anti-Slavery Society. He has attended, during the past few days, several meetings in Dublin, at one of which the Lord Mayor presided, and he will this week deliver a lecture in Waterford, on the subject of American slavery ... Mr Douglass is a highly gifted speaker, as we perceive from the reports of his lectures in the Dublin journals; he evidently possesses a cultivated mind, and is most assiduous in adding to his stores of information. We sincerely trust that a Waterford public will show an interest in this matter, adequate to its high import; and that the sale of his *Narrative*, which can be had of the author, hugely interesting and important as it is, will testify the active sympathy they entertain for the trampled down and oppressed bond slave.

Another local paper, meanwhile, the staunchly O'Connellite *Chronicle and Munster Advertiser*, was in the midst of a dispute with the *Boston Pilot* over the Irish American response to slavery, deploring how 'almost every shabby and eliminated Irishman, immediately that he leaves his own bog and potatoes, becomes a most ardent admirer of this nasty 'institution''. The *Pilot* took offence at this attack, arguing that the Irish in America hated 'slavery and tyranny' but felt 'too humble and too *new*' in the country to lead any campaign on the issue. It also insisted that reality of slavery was not as bad as portrayed in the British and Irish press.

Edited by Cavan-born Patrick Donahoe, the *Boston Pilot* was the leading Irish American newspaper of the period. Although generally pro-O'Connell, like a lot of the Liberator's supporters in America, it was uncomfortable with the constant attacks on slavery coming from Ireland. In the midst of its war of words with the Waterford paper, the following appeared:

We are sick to surfeit of the continued attacks which are made upon this country at Conciliation Hall, by injudicious and unwise men connected with the cause. It can serve no purpose if they split the dome of that patriot Hall with denunciation . . . and . . . it does immense mischief to the popular enterprise here. We are not surprised that Mr John O'Connell [the Liberator's son and political heir], in his ardent love of the human races, should magnify the blot of slavery upon our national escutcheon. But, humble as we are, we could tell him that if he purposes for himself the task of liberating the whole world, and to take its sins and wrongs and injuries and power in the same budget as Repeal, and that he will not be content with the purification of one without the whole, he had better at once tell the people of Ireland that the Millennium is the period of attaining Repeal.

Emancipation of the slaves would be achieved far quicker, the paper claimed, without foreign interference, while expressions like 'O, base America!' only served to harm the Irish in the country.

The *Chronicle*, however, owned and edited by Cornelius Redmond, a future mayor of

Waterford city, continued its attack. 'Is there no reminiscence of suffering, of oppression, of slavery in Ireland? Ah, no. They learn the slave cant of the *free* land — they love what the Yankee loves, and hate what he hates . . . and Ireland being out of sight, she is called presumptuous and offensive for reminding the heretofore sons of her bogs, her mountains and her valleys, that they are going on in an unnatural career.' Other papers got involved, with the *Kilkenny Journal* supporting the *Chronicle*. With so many local journals discussing the question of slavery in heightened terms, the scene seemed set for a large turnout at Douglass's talk.

This, however, was not to be.

'*Shame on Ye, Heartless Men of Waterford*'
'On Thursday evening, Mr Douglass, who, as our readers have already been informed, was but recently an American slave, and who is even now liable, should he come within the jurisdiction of his former masters, or their confreres in guilt, to be again subjected to their tender mercies — the fetter, and the lash, delivered a lecture on the subject of slavery, in a large room of the Town Hall,' wrote the *Waterford Mail*. 'Notwithstanding the unfavourable state of the weather, and the

172

short notice which the public had received of the intended meeting, we were glad to perceive that the attendance was both numerous and respectable. Mr Douglass, whose manner is highly prepossessing, delivered himself with energy and feeling, and was listened to with marked attention by his auditory, whose sympathies he excited by his faithful telling of the black man's suffering and the black man's wrongs . . . The cause he so ably advocates deserves the support of every friend to humanity — of every Christian, no matter what their denomination.'

This claim of a large attendance, however, was rather undone by the publication of a (not especially good) poem in the same paper a few days later.

To the People of Waterford
On their Chilling Reception of Frederick Douglass

Shame on ye, heartless men of Waterford!
Who, when the slave come to your hearth
    and home
To thrill your bosoms with his lightning
    word
Doubtfully question, 'Wherefore does he
    come?'

What unto us the woes of cat and cord?
Of life extinguished, or of soul held dumb?
To, give us rest and peace, our gentle ears
Soothe with bland murmurs, if you speak
    of wrong.

We're delicate. Mayhap our exquisite tears
Should start if troubled by your 'lan-
    guage strong'!
Must Douglass shrink from truth to still
    your fears?
Deny the cruel torture felt so long?

Blind, craven men! Slaves, slaves in heart
    and brain!
Your <u>souls</u> are dark — your minds con-
    fess the chain

'He did not come to the right place,' wrote the *Mail*'s local rival, the *Chronicle*, rather self-servingly of Douglass's talk. 'If he had given intimation of his coming at The Chronicle Office, we should have made the city hear of him.'

There was an interest in anti-slavery in Waterford, a city with significant Quaker interests like Jacobs, the biscuit makers, and Malcolmsons, the millers and shipbuilders. (It was also home to another famous Quaker school in Newtown.) Indeed, when Remond visited a few years earlier, delivering five successful lectures, the numbers seeking admission had been so large that the organisers started to charge for the last few talks to keep the venues manageable. There had been a charge for Douglass's talk, too, and this has been put forward, together with the bad weather and the fact that there were popular horse races in nearby Tramore at the same time, as reasons for the disappointing response.

There would be no such ambiguity about the extent of Douglass's welcome at his next destination — Cork.

8

'The Good City of Cork'

By the time Frederick Douglass, James Buffum and Richard D. Webb arrived in Cork, they had been each other's constant companions for almost six weeks. Webb had tired of Douglass, whom he described as 'absurdly haughty, self-possessed and prone to take offence' in a letter to Maria Weston Chapman, a principal lieutenant of William Lloyd Garrison's in Boston. According to Webb, it had actually been Douglass's 'insolent' behaviour towards Buffum that first set him against the celebrated escaped slave. There was certainly some tension between the two Americans, Buffum leaving Cork before Douglass and travelling over to England. He would meet the Hutchinsons in Liverpool, shocking them with the news that he had had a 'falling out' with Douglass, and 'could not stay with him any longer'. It is difficult to apportion blame. Perhaps Webb's judgements were correct, and Douglass was acting in an egotistical, high-handed manner with those around him. Or was the falling-out simply the result of the friction that can arise between any two people thrown together for a long period of time? Douglass and Buffum, it must be remembered, were acquaintances rather than close friends before the tour. It is also possible that deeper animosities were at work, as it may have been around this time that Douglass discovered abolitionists in America had been plying Webb with letters urging him to keep a close eye on the escaped slave, the suggestion from Chapman that he might be tempted to abandon the American Anti-Slavery Society for the more financially powerful British and Foreign Anti-Slavery Society provoking a particularly furious response. Was Buffum, then, the unfortunate, near-at-hand target of the ire Douglass felt for the white Boston abolitionist grandees?

Whatever the cause, Douglass and Buffum would be reunited when the tour moved on to Britain in early 1846, spending six months travelling together through Scotland and England. Douglass, in fact, would be grateful to Buffum for agreeing to look after some of his family affairs when the Lynn man returned home that summer, Douglass staying on in Britain until the following spring. The two men were still corresponding in friendly terms decades later, Buffum thanking Douglass for a 'sweet little note' that 'revived in memory those long years of trial and conflict which you and I spent together in this country and in the old world'.

Webb would probably have been quite happy to have had nothing more to do with Douglass after parting with him in Cork. This was not possible, however, with letters to Douglass from abolitionists and family in America routinely directed to Webb's address. There was also the not inconsequential matter of the *Narrative*. It was selling well, the initial run of 2,000 copies almost sold out by Christmas. According to Webb's calculations, sales from the first Dublin edition of the book must have made Douglass at least $750, more than enough to help defray the costs of the trip. Talks were soon under way about a second edition, which would be printed in early 1846. Against Webb's wishes, Douglass insisted that letters of support from two Presbyterian ministers in Ireland should be included in the preface to the new edition. Webb, more attuned than Douglass to the religious sensitivities of the Irish, had wanted to avoid anything that gave the book a sectarian appearance. Douglass, however, saw their inclusion as a way of proving that he was not the irreligious agitator some opponents tried to depict.

A number of writers have portrayed this assertiveness surrounding the publication of the second Dublin edition of the *Narrative* as a sign of the growing sense of self-confidence the Irish tour had given Douglass. There is some truth to this, but it should not be forgotten what strength of character it took for Douglass to first step onto an abolitionist platform in America. He had never been a meek or timid personality, nor was he ever afraid to give offence if he thought himself to be in the right.

'The Affection of Every One of Us'

Chapman received far more positive reports about Douglass from Isabel Jennings, the daughter of the Unitarian family with whom Douglass stayed in Cork. Douglass was a 'noble-minded' man who immediately felt 'like a friend'. Buffum, too, before he left, was much admired in the city. Despite the warm welcome, both men, Jennings wrote, were suffering somewhat, having felt 'the dampness of the climate very much'. The weather had certainly been terrible, constant rain helping the spread of the potato blight. 'It has descended into the earth and is eating away the poor man's life while its leprous spots fester in his food,' wrote the *Southern Reporter*. 'The farmer looks over his fields and sees the external appearance of soundness and abundance. He is happy in the supposition that his land is free and his plantings undiseased. But when he comes to try them and cuts into the core, he finds the murrain has entered deeply, and his hopes of provision for his family, his cattle and his rent are blasted and destroyed.'

As co-secretary of the Cork Ladies Anti-Slavery Society, the 32-year-old Isabel Jennings was a regular correspondent of Chapman's, especially around the time of the annual Boston Bazaar. 'Again we have the pleasure of sending through you, to the American Anti-Slavery Society, some articles for the Fair to be held in Boston,' a typical letter began. 'Many questions are asked as to whether plain or fancy work would be preferred? Little things for children or knitted . . . articles? We would be glad to hear as many would do either with equal pleasure.' Showing that even good-hearted abolitionists were not beyond a little tax evasion, Jennings informed Chapman on one occasion that, in order to save on duties, the prices on the items sent over had been marked at one third of what they were expected to fetch. 'We were afraid to put too low a price lest suspicions might be aroused.' There were also times when Jennings had to apologise for the poor quality of some of the material dispatched across the Atlantic, one elderly lady donating 'a parcel of old linen'. Nevertheless, she felt it was better to send these items over than offend the donors.

Thomas Jennings, Isabel's father, was the owner of a successful company manufacturing vinegar, magnesia, mineral oil and non-alcoholic beverages like soda water. He had set it up in the early part of the century. Business, however, was just one strand to this man's rich, multifaceted life. He had published some (pretty poor) poetry in the 1820s, inspired, he told the editor of *Blackwood's Magazine*, by the death of the famous Irish boxer 'Sir' Dan Donnelly. He may also have lectured on phrenology in the 1830s. Jennings was certainly involved in any number of local groups, such as the Royal Cork Institution, together with broader humanitarian concerns like temperance and anti-slavery. His business partner, Richard Dowden, was of a similarly active and philanthropic ilk, immersed in temperance, repeal, anti-slavery and a multitude of local boards and societies. The 51-year-old Dowden, who had studied medicine before being approached by the Jennings family to manage their business, had even published a poem, again on Dan Donnelly, in the same issue of *Blackwood's*. He was the Lord Mayor at the time of Douglass's visit.

Jennings was a wealthy man and respected member of the city's business community. His success, however, had not stilled his strong sense of justice; something of his character can be gleaned from the fact that he was in the magistrate's court the day Douglass arrived in Cork, having brought charges against two police officers he had seen dragging a prisoner along the streets, banging the man's head and back against the kerbstones. The two officers, Sub-Constables Finucane and Ford, had in turn accused Jennings of inciting a crowd to rescue the prisoner, John Callaghan. The magistrates, to Jennings's chagrin, dropped the whole case, albeit with some condescending remarks about being sure he acted out of humanitarian concerns.

Thomas Jennings lived with his wife, Ann, and their eight grown-up children in a large house on Brown Street, an area near the Huguenot Quarter which was demolished in the 1970s to make way for a shopping centre car park. They were just a few yards away from St Patrick's Street, the city's main thoroughfare, where bookshops such as Purcell & Co. and Bradford & Co. sold Douglass's *Narrative*. They were also quite close to Cork's famous English Market and its myriad stalls selling every cut of meat imaginable. The Jenningses also owned land to the west of the city, part of which would soon be acquired by the newly established Queen's College Cork (present-day University College Cork). As befitted a family of Unitarians, a faith shared by John Quincy Adams, Louisa May Alcott, Ralph Waldo Emerson and Mary Wollstonecraft, the house on Brown Street was an extremely open-minded place, full of music, gossip and talk of the latest reforms. Isabel's sister Jane was another prominent member of the Cork Ladies Anti-Slavery Society. A brother, Francis, meanwhile, was a member of the Royal Irish Academy and author of numerous pamphlets on Irish social and economic issues. Douglass delighted in the free flow of talk and ideas around the Jenningses' living room, the three weeks in Brown Street a personal highlight of his two-year tour of Great Britain and Ireland. (They certainly seem to have provided him with much more vivid company than Webb and his extended Quaker clan.) The admiration was shared. 'We are', Jane Jennings wrote to Chapman soon after Douglass's departure, 'a large family, my mother, three brothers and five sisters, generally considered not easily pleased — but Frederick won the affection of every one of us.'

'A Girdle of Anti-Slavery Fire'

Although he does not seem to have made a speech on the occasion, Douglass's first public appearance in Cork came at a soirée

183

held to mark Fr Mathew's birthday at the Temperance Institute on Academy Street on Friday 10 October. (This was a separate event to the soirée Mathew would hold for Douglass ten days later.) He may even have been whisked there as soon as he got off the coach from Waterford (stopping, perhaps, to give a short talk in Youghal en route). It was a big affair, with temperance bands parading through the streets beforehand, accompanied by flaming torches and tar barrels. There were fireworks, more music and dancing back at the Institute. The guest of honour, Fr Mathew, retired not long after nine o'clock. The remainder of the party, however, stayed on until the early hours of the next morning, the fact that it was a teetotal affair, with tea, fruits and confectionary served to guests, in no way quelling the enthusiasm of the revellers.

Douglass would give a talk on temperance a couple of nights later, at the Globe Lane Temperance Hall near the bottom of Barrack Street. This was the second in a series of twelve public lectures he would deliver in the city over the course of three weeks. (He had intended to stay for only ten days but enjoyed himself too much.) The *Cork Examiner* carried a short notice of the speech, impressed with Douglass's 'calm, forcible manner' and 'frequent bursts of fervid eloquence'. That such a man 'should ever have been held as the property of another, his noble frame tasked, flogged and fettered, and his active, intelligent and expressive mind cramped and darkened' was a disgraceful indictment of the slave system. The paper was confident Douglass would speak just as ably on slavery as he did on temperance, promising its readers a 'happy intellectual treat' should they attend his talk at the city courthouse the next day, an advertisement for which was located in a neighbouring column. Admittance was free, the gallery reserved for ladies.

Although Douglass gave a short, regrettably unrecorded talk to the Cork Anti-Slavery Society almost as soon as he arrived in the city, it was his appearance at the courthouse on the afternoon of Tuesday 14 October that really introduced him to the people of Cork. The building was 'densely crowded in every part' long before the meeting was scheduled to begin, with more than 100 ladies sitting close together in the gallery. Mayor Dowden, who, like his close friends and fellow Unitarians the Jenningses, would be a constant presence during Douglass's stay in Cork, presided over the meeting. A series of anti-slavery resolutions were passed before

Douglass finally stepped forward to address the large audience, with a two-hour speech entitled 'I am Here to Spread Light on American Slavery'.

'I stand before you in the most extraordinary position that one human being ever stood before his race — a slave,' Douglass announced starkly. 'A slave not in the ordinary sense of the term, not in the political sense, but in its real and intrinsic meaning. I have not been stripped of one of my rights and privileges, but of all. By the laws of the country whence I came, I was deprived of myself — of my own body, soul and spirit, and I am free only because I succeeded in escaping the clutches of the man who claimed me as his property.'

Douglass spoke briefly of his years lecturing in America and of the decision to publish his autobiography. 'The excitement at last increased so much that it was thought better for me to get out of the way lest my master might use some stratagem to get me back into his clutches.' He drew gasps from the crowd when he described how he bore the 'marks of the slave-driver's whip' on his back, would carry them to his grave. Much worse, however, than any physical pain was the manner in which slavery crushed the spirit of its victims, slaveholders enjoying the 'bloody power of tearing asunder those whom God had joined together — of separating husband from wife, parent from child, and of leaving the hut vacant and the hearth desolate'.

Quoting again Theodore Dwight Weld's great book, *American Slavery As It Is*, he listed some of the punishments set down in law for slaves: 'If more than seven slaves are found together in any road, without a white person — *twenty lashes apiece*. For visiting a plantation without a written pass — *ten lashes*. For letting loose a boat from where it is made fast — *thirty-nine lashes*; and for the second offence, shall have his ear cut off. For having an article for sale without a ticket from his master — *ten lashes*. For being on horseback without the written permission of his master — *twenty-five lashes*.' He also described how he had seen one poor woman who had her ear nailed to a post, for attempting to run away. 'The agony she endured was so great, that she tore away, and left her ear behind.'

Douglass, in the words of the *Examiner*, next 'tore the mask off the religious cant of those dealers in human flesh, the Wesleyans and Episcopalians in America . . . who preached from their pulpits the most atrocious doctrines justifying the system of slavery, and who perverted the sacred word of God to the base purpose of human oppression'.

'In America, Bibles and slaveholders go hand in hand,' Douglass declared powerfully. 'The Church and the slave prison stand together, and while you hear the chanting of psalms in one, you hear the clanking of chains in the other; the man who wields the cowhide during the week, fills the pulpit on Sunday. Here we have robbery and religion united — devils dressed in angels garments.'

Douglass went on to treat the rapt audience to his stock impersonation of a Southern minister. More seriously, however, he also explained, amid constant waves of applause, how the Irish could help put an end to slavery by lending the moral and religious influence they had over the American Churches to the abolitionist cause. 'We want to awaken the slaveholder to a sense of the iniquity of his position ... We want to encircle America with a girdle of anti-slavery fire ... We want Methodists in Ireland to speak to those of America, and say, 'While your hands are red with blood, while the thumb screws and gags and whips are wrapped up in the pontifical robes of your Church, we will have no fellowship with you, or acknowledge you as Christians.''

Douglass sat down to a standing ovation. The city was convinced.

'The Blacks across the Sea are Very Precious'

Douglass's lecture at the courthouse had actually been preceded by an 'anti-slavery breakfast' at Lloyd's Hotel on George's Street (present-day Oliver Plunkett Street). Hosted by the Cork Anti-Slavery Society, this was a small, select affair, with members of the society and local dignitaries getting to spend some time with Douglass at close quarters. The collection for the Boston Bazaar was mentioned and Douglass made a short speech. It is likely that some copies of the *Narrative* were sold, perhaps even signed by the famous author. The Cork Anti-Slavery Society was used to such gatherings; the papers of Richard Dowden are replete with notes connected to the appearance of anti-slavery speakers in the city. These included Richard Robert Madden, Charles Lenox Remond and Moses Roper, the latter an escaped slave and author like Douglass, albeit less remembered.

Cork had a long history of anti-slavery activity, the Quaker influence once again looming large. In the mid- to late 1700s, for

189

example, Samuel Neale, a prominent Quaker merchant in the city, had acted as a link between the American Quaker anti-slavery activist Anthony Benezet and the Irish statesman and philosopher Edmund Burke when Benezet was trying to get British parliamentary action on the slave trade. (Although not a Quaker, Burke had been educated at the famous Ballitore School, maintaining lifelong friendships with Quakers like Richard Shackleton, a son of Abraham Shackleton, the founder of the school.) Then, in 1792, a Cork printer called Anthony Edwards published a pamphlet on the horrors of the slave trade, one of the myriad local efforts that, replicated throughout Great Britain and Ireland, would help end the slave trade in 1807.

In January 1826 the Cork Anti-Slavery Society was formed by Joshua Beale, an elderly Quaker who had decided to devote the remaining years of his life to the campaign to abolish slavery in the West Indies. It was a broad-based group, Catholics, Protestants, Quakers and other Nonconformists coming together in common cause. Despite the traditional Quaker distaste for secular political activism, Abraham Beale, another Quaker member of the Cork Anti-Slavery Society, urged voters at an 1830 by-election to support only those candidates pledged to anti-slavery. A number of petitions were also sent to parliament and, in something of an early precursor to the fair-trade movement, a shop was set up in Cork selling sweets made from Indian rather than West Indian sugar. One local newspaper derided the 'good-natured jellies, warm-hearted ices, amiable tarts . . . and philanthropic lozenges'. Nevertheless, all the talk of anti-slavery was a cause of concern for those with business interests in the West Indies; the port of Cork still enjoyed substantial trading links with the Caribbean. They argued that the slaves were well treated and quite happy until outsiders started interfering on their behalf.

The Cork Anti-Slavery Society continued to meet after the abolition of slavery in the West Indies in 1833, turning their attention to the system of 'apprenticeship' in the West Indies and then slavery in the American South. One member, Mary B. Tuckey, even published a short book of anti-slavery poems called *The Wrongs of Africa*. The Quaker input remained strong, leading to some tart observations that 'though they would not care a pin for us whites or our liberties yet the blacks across the sea are very precious'. However, leadership of the society had started to move to Independents (also known as Congregationalists) and Unitarians like the Jenningses and Dowden. It was also around this time that the Cork Ladies Anti-Slavery Society came to the fore, meeting in the library of Independent Chapel on George's Street every Saturday morning.

Newspaper reports of Douglass's speeches in Ireland always made sure to reference the 'crowded' female galleries or 'numerous' ladies present. This condescending approach was de rigueur for the time. Women, however, played a genuinely instrumental role in the anti-slavery movement on both sides of the Atlantic, stepping out of their supposed private 'sphere' to provide formidable leaders like Lucretia Mott and Abigail Kelley as well as the 'great silent army' of volunteers and fundraisers. Nevertheless, it cannot be denied that Douglass was particularly well known for inspiring something close to devotion in women's groups. He was a brilliant, charismatic speaker and a powerfully attractive man. As his biographer William McFeely has noted, there was always a great deal of prurient speculation — not always devoid of racism — about the sexual component of Douglass's friendships with white women. Isabel Jennings, however, to whom Douglass became very close, was quick to quash any hints of impropriety about his behaviour in

Ireland, writing to Chapman that he 'evinced the highest regard for his wife and children' at all times and avoided 'confidential conversations with young ladies', even though one or two were 'rather absurd in their over-attention'. Webb, rather callously, later wondered how Douglass would be able to bear the sight of his wife after all the 'petting' he received from elegant women in Britain and Ireland.

Douglass was always much more comfortable opening up to women than to men, something McFeely traces back to his relationship with his grandmother Betsey Bailey. When he decided to prolong his overseas tour, it was to 'Dear Isa' — Isabel Jennings — that Douglass confided, worrying about how much the delay would pain his wife Anna. The relationship between Jennings and Douglass trailed off somewhat in the 1850s, especially after he hired the white English reformer Julia Griffiths to run his new newspaper in America. Isabel was convinced Griffiths read all her letters to Douglass and became much more guarded. Rumours of an affair — never proven — between Douglass and Griffiths were also widespread at this time. 'I am sure,' Isabel wrote caustically, 'he thinks anti-slavery zeal is the strongest emotion she is capable of.'

This frostiness lay in the future. In Cork in October 1845 Isabel was more than happy accompanying Douglass to the many lectures he still had to give around the city.

'Their Pulpits Became Silent'
Douglass was at the Wesleyan Chapel on St Patrick's Street on Friday 17 October, delivering another substantial, two-hour lecture on how 'Slavery Corrupts American Society and Religion'. It was uncomfortable listening for some of the Methodist ministers and Quakers in the crowd.

Slavery, Douglass began, spread a 'dark cloud' over the so-called 'land of liberty', its corrupting influence nowhere clearer than in the religious organisations of the country. The Quakers, he regretted to say, the split at the Indiana Yearly Meeting still clearly in mind, had turned their backs on a proud anti-slavery history. Instead of being despised by the 'inhuman traffickers', as had formerly been the case, they were now spoken of by slaveholders as an 'excellent body'. Douglass's criticisms seem harsh given the continued deep involvement of so many Quakers in the anti-slavery movement and Underground Railroad, not to mention the support he had received from that body in Ireland. Nevertheless, anything less than the most whole-hearted commitment to abolition was always

194

a failure in his eyes.

'The Methodists of the Episcopal church had also started on the high principle of opposition to the slavery system,' Douglass continued. 'Whilst their body was in its infancy it adhered scrupulously to the principle, but when it extended itself, and when slaveholders intermarried with its members, they succeeded in rooting out the noble sentiments of humanity, and the moment the clergyman's salary became dependent on the voice of the slaveholder, eked by him from the toil and sweat of the bondsman, that moment their pulpits became silent.'

Douglass turned next to the Presbyterians, who justified support of slavery by reference to Philemon 1:10–16, where St Paul returns the runaway slave Onesimus to his master. 'And yet these men, who scourged and branded feeble women until they were saturated in their own blood, and who plundered the cradles of helpless infancy, these were the men who sent out missionaries to evangelise the world, and who turned their eyes to heaven to thank God that they lived in a land of religion.'

'The Baptist church, which extended from end to end of America, equally supported and countenanced the system,' Douglass then declared. 'At their last meeting in Baltimore Dr Johnson, a man-thief, preached the sermon, whilst another man-thief read the prayers, and the congregation of slaveholders, women floggers and cradle-plunderers all sang — 'Lord what a pleasing sight; we brothers all agree.''

Douglass was referring here to the Baptist Triennial Convention in Baltimore in late April 1841. Alert to accusations of exaggeration, all such references to the American Churches and their gatherings were scrupulously based on facts, often taken from books like Weld's *American Slavery As It Is* and James G. Birney's *The American Churches: The Bulwarks of American Slavery*. Douglass returned to Weld to provide his audience with examples of advertisements for runaway slaves that left little doubt as to the cruelty of the slaveholders. 'Ran away a Negro girl called Mary — has a small scar over her eye, a good many teeth missing — the letter A is branded on her cheek and forehead.' 'Ran away a Negro woman and two children — a few days before she went off, I burned her with a hot iron on the left side of her face — I tried to make the letter M.'

At the end of the speech, a number of Methodist ministers rose to voice their anger at Douglass's attacks on their Church. William Reilly pointed out the role Methodists had played in abolishing slavery in the

West Indies while a Joseph W. McKay accused Douglass of attacking Methodists in his courthouse speech just to raise easy cheers from the mainly Catholic audience present that day. Douglass replied that he had been speaking of the Methodist Church in America rather than in Britain and Ireland, adding somewhat disingenuously with reference to the courthouse that 'it would be requiring too much that he should know men's religion by their faces'. However, he also warned against any defence of the Methodists in America, noting some 'over-sensitiveness on the part of . . . persons which induced them to curl up when any charge was laid to their co-religionists of another country'. His rebuttal, the *Southern Reporter* wrote, was well received and Douglass resumed his seat 'amid loud applause'.

The *Southern Reporter* and *Cork Examiner* were very supportive of Douglass during his stay in the city — the more conservative *Cork Constitution* somewhat less so. The Cork papers of this period were representative of the wider provincial press: four-page affairs, with occasional two-page supplements, costing about 5d. They followed a fairly consistent style. The *Examiner* had seven columns in each page. It began with a page and a half of advertisements, public notices (births, marriages, etc.), shipping news, share prices and prospectuses for the myriad new railway companies being registered, most of which never amounted to anything, the British Isles being on the whole in the grip of something of a 'railway mania'. A few columns of editorials were then followed by two pages of more advertisements together with local, national and international news. The latter, lifted in the main from the English press, was generally of the sensationalist 'Horrible Murder in Montevideo' fare. Everything was in extremely small print, and at times of big Repeal meetings, almost the entire paper could be given over to coverage of Daniel O'Connell.

The pro-Douglass stance of the *Examiner* and *Reporter* saw them praised in a resolution passed at Douglass's last anti-slavery meeting in Cork.

'A Heart Swelling With Gratitude'
Over the last two weeks of October, Douglass would deliver anti-slavery addresses at venues including the Temperance Institute, St Patrick's Temperance Hall and, most notably, the Imperial Hotel on the South Mall, the ubiquitous Dowden presiding most of the time. His audiences were usually characterised as belonging

to the most 'respectable' sections of society. Nevertheless, his influence went deeper, the *Cork Examiner* writing approvingly of how the 'suffering poor' were 'thronging' to hear him speak. Although there was some natural overlap in the speeches, Douglass made great efforts to keep his audiences interested and engaged, working on new angles and themes all the time, extending his intellectual range and moving well beyond personal testimony and victimhood. He was also extremely adept at moulding his speeches to the different audiences, heaping effusive praise on O'Connell before the city courthouse crowd but not mentioning him once at the Wesleyan Chapel.

Douglass's final public appearance in Cork came at a farewell soirée on Monday 3 November, held at the Independent Chapel. Ralph Varian, the secretary of the Cork Anti-Slavery Society who would be imprisoned a few years later with his brother Isaac for their part in the Young Ireland rebellion, read from a long 'Address to Frederick Douglass'. Douglass was praised for his efforts in support of the 'holy cause' while Charles Lenox Remond was still 'affectionately remembered'. A local poet, Daniel Casey, wrote the following verse:

Stranger from a distant nation,
We welcome thee with acclamation,

And, as a brother warmly greet thee —
Rejoiced in Erin's Isle to meet thee

Then *Cead Mille Failthe* to the stranger,
Free from bondage, chains and danger.
Who could have heard thy hapless story,
Of tyrants — canting, base and gory;
Whose heart throbbed not with deep
    pulsation
For the trampled slaves emancipation.

Oh! why should different hue or feature
Prevent the sacred laws of Nature,
And every tie of feeling sever? —
The voice of Nature thunders 'Never!'

Then borne o'er the Atlantic waters
The cry of Erin's sons and daughters
For freedom shall henceforth be blended
Till Slavery's hellish reign be ended.

Other poems and songs celebrating Douglass
were composed around this time, some of
which Isabel Jennings forwarded to Maria
Weston Chapman in Boston for publication
in the abolitionist press. She also asked
Chapman to send the poems to Douglass's
illiterate wife, Anna. 'He says that though she
cannot read them she will love to look on
them.'

Douglass left Cork a few days later, writing a letter to Dowden from Limerick.

My Dear Sir,
Allow me to express to you as well as words can, my deep sense of the obligations I am under to yourself for the many attentions which you were pleased to show me during my somewhat protracted stay in the City of which you are the highly honoured chief executive officer.

I think I am too well acquainted with the motives that guided you in your kind offices toward me — for a moment to suppose you desirous of such an expression from me. Indeed I know you require no such expression at my hand and I am therefore the more anxious to do it — not . . . for the purposes of rewarding you . . . I do it my Dear Sir, to ease a heart swelling with gratitude.

I have travelled a great deal during the last few years — and have met with many benefactors but never have I met with one, in your station, having so many public cares and weighty responsibilities to bear, and yet so ready, so willing and anxious to devote time talent and official influence to the advancement of the noblest objects as yourself.

I speak just what I feel — and what all who are acquainted with the facts will confess to be true, when I say that to yours and the deep interest which the Miss Jennings took in me and my mission, I am almost entirely indebted for the success which attended my humble efforts while in the good City of Cork.

I shall ever remember my visit with pleasure, and never shall I think of Cork without remembering that yourself and the kind friends just named constituted the source from whence flowed much of the light, life and warmth of humanity which I found in that good City.

It seems that Dowden had made a gift of a ring to Douglass, who wrote: 'I received the token of your esteem which you sent, I have it on the little finger of my right hand, I never wore one, or had the disposition to do so before, I shall wear this, and prize it as the representative of the holy feelings with which you espoused and advocated my humble cause.'

Dowden had clearly enjoyed his time with Douglass, guiding him around the churches and meeting houses of the city. Nevertheless, there had still been some official duties to attend to, what Douglass called Dowden's 'public cares and weighty responsibilities'. These included a letter sent to the Lord Lieutenant on the 'very great and it is to be feared well-founded alarm which the decay of the potato crop' had produced among the people of Cork.

9

'This Persecuted Son of Africa'

'The rot of the potato continues to so engross the public mind that scarcely any other topic is discussed in the press, at public meetings, in the news rooms, or in private circles.' So wrote the *Limerick Reporter* a few days before Frederick Douglass arrived in the city, adding fearfully, 'there is no knowing where the ravages of this rot will stop'. It was certainly the main topic on the front page of the newspaper, where the proceedings of a meeting of the Mansion House Committee, a high-profile relief organisation headed by the Duke of Leinster and Lord Cloncurry, vied for space with suggestions from correspondents on how to make use of diseased potatoes. Dr Daniel Cahill, a Catholic priest and one of the most popular science lecturers of the day, had dipped some partially diseased potatoes into a strong potassium solution, leaving them to boil for ten minutes. 'On taking them out I found a glutinous matter oozing from the potatoes in the diseased parts, a fact which convinced me that the potash [potassium solution] had united with the acid, and was drawing it to the surface. On the potatoes being perfectly cooled I found the diseased part had lost its offensive smell, its watery character, and had assumed a yellowish appearance, and, above all, had acquired a floury texture. The disease seemed to have been sucked out by the potash ... and those potatoes ... were perfectly healthy.' The intrepid Cahill had also soaked some slightly diseased potatoes in a solution of urine and river water. These too, he declared, were 'perfectly fit for use'. He had eaten them for dinner.

An article copied from the *Gardener's Chronicle*, meanwhile, came complete with a diagram for a potato-grinding machine, which could be used to get starch out of diseased potatoes. According to the group of Scientific Commissioners dispatched by the Tory Prime Minister Sir Robert Peel to report on the crisis in Ireland, this was the best use that could be made of the most seriously blighted potatoes, as the starch, although inedible by itself, could be mixed with flour to make good bread. 'A machine of this kind is easily and quickly made, and costs comparatively little,' stated the *Chronicle*, the leading horticultural journal in England whose editor, the well-respected botanist Dr John Lindley, was a member of the Scientific Commission.

Amidst this surfeit of articles on the potato crisis, the reader of the *Limerick Reporter* could also find news of the calling to the bar of Charles Gavan Duffy, editor of *The Nation* and later a prominent rebel, and of the sentencing to seven years' transportation of two Limerick brothers, William and Denis Gallaher, who had been found guilty of stealing pigs from a neighbour. There was also a brief note on the construction of the Limerick — Waterford railway. More than 300 men were already employed on the Limerick side, a figure expected to rise to 2,000 by the following summer. It was a project that would certainly be of great benefit to the labourers and tradesmen of the city in the desperate years to come.

'A Labyrinth of Busy Swarming Poverty'
With the rail network still in its infancy, Douglass would have travelled to Limerick by the traditional coach route, through towns and villages like Mallow, Charleville, Kilmallock and Bruff. This was good farming country, the east of Limerick lying right at the heart of the Golden Vale, Ireland's premier dairying terrain. Further west, around Rathkeale and Newcastle West, then the two most

populous towns outside the city, the quality of land deteriorated and the structure of farming changed. The emphasis was on tillage and turf cutting, and there was a preponderance of smaller farms. Despite being generally poorer than their eastern counterparts, the farmers of the west were considered to be fairer men, old poems and songs like 'The Galbally Farmer' deriding the stinginess of wealthy east Limerick farmers.

Douglass was travelling on his own for the first time, Richard D. Webb having returned to Dublin after just a few days in Cork and a disgruntled James Buffum attending a large Anti-Corn Law League meeting in Manchester. The Corn Laws — whose putative repeal were causing great controversy across Britain — were a set of prohibitive duties that had been placed on imported corn since the end of the Napoleonic Wars. A perennial source of debate, they returned to the top of the political agenda during the mid-1840s, against a backdrop of economic distress across Britain and Ireland. Opponents of the duties, including the middle-class pressure group the Anti-Corn Law League and the recently established *Economist* magazine, blamed them for keeping the price of bread artificially high to the exclusive benefit of large (often Tory) landowners. Supporters, known as Protectionists, argued that the Corn Laws protected British farmers from having their produce undercut by cheap foreign imports. The Protectionists joined forces with some tenant farmers to present themselves as defenders of traditional rural society. The question of repeal, therefore, became a proxy for any number of overlapping debates: Protectionism versus free trade, the aristocracy versus the people, rural versus urban.

American abolitionists like Buffum and William Lloyd Garrison, who gave Anti-Corn Law League meetings a good deal of coverage in *The Liberator*, saw the campaign as yet another manifestation of the 'spirit of reform' that seemed to be characteristic of the age. Others developed an economic critique in which the Corn Laws played a central role in upholding slavery, by excluding free-grown American corn while allowing the untrammelled importation of slave-grown cotton. Within Ireland, too, the Corn Law issue was widely discussed, taking on even greater urgency in light of the potato failure. Newspapers like the *Limerick Reporter* urged the opening of the ports to cheaper foreign grain as a means of alleviating hardship. Peel, who had served as Chief Secretary for Ireland from 1812-18, knew first-hand how potato failure led to distress in the country. Although he ignored appeals from Daniel O'Connell and others for a ban on distillation using grain and a temporary suspension of grain exports from Ireland, his thinking influenced in part by a belief that the shortage would be temporary, he did establish a Relief Commission to organise food depots and co-ordinate local relief committees. Legislation was also passed to finance public relief works, mainly on roads and drainage schemes, on which locals could be employed. Circumventing parliamentary and public opposition to giving aid to Ireland, Peel even organised the secret shipment of £100,000 worth of maize (Indian meal) into the country, which was parcelled out to depots run by the army Commissariat and Coast Guard. He was also coming around to the idea of repealing the Corn Laws, although this predated the Irish crisis.

Protectionism was assumed to be a central tenet of the governing Tory party policy. Privately, however, the Prime Minister had long held doubts about the value of the Corn Laws. Indications of Peel's weakening resolve began to seep out into the public arena and the debate grew ever more strident. Powerful voices including the writers Thomas Carlyle and Charles Dickens came out in support of repeal. Dickens wove the free-trade ideas of the Anti-Corn Law League into *The Chimes*, his tale of a starving farm labourer, Will Fern, and a tyrannical landlord, Sir Joseph Bowley. (*The Chimes* was Dickens's second Christmas book, but did not match the success of its predecessor, *A Christmas Carol*.) The Protectionists hit back with a propaganda machine of their own, backed by magazines like *Blackwood's* and *Fraser's*, and both sides held mass rallies and mobilised forces across the country.

Against this backdrop, *The Times* of 4 December 1845 stunned readers with the announcement of Peel's final conversion to repeal. 'The decision . . . is no longer a secret. Parliament, it is confidently reported, is to be summoned for the first week in January; and the Royal Speech will . . . recommend an immediate consideration of the Corn Laws, preparatory to their total repeal.' John Bright, MP for Durham and one of the leading opponents of the Corn Laws, was so excited that he was inspired to write that 'the reading of the article has almost made me ill — what a glorious prospect is now before us'. Less glorious was the reaction within Tory ranks, the party splitting irreparably between Protectionists and Peelites. With his Cabinet divided, Peel offered his resignation to Queen Victoria. The Whig opposition, however, under Lord John Russell, proved unable to form a government. Peel was forced to stay in place and see the measure through, and the Corn Laws were finally repealed in June 1846. However, it would be another three years before the change was implemented fully, and despite the hopes of writers in the *Limerick Reporter* and other papers, the contribution of Corn Laws repeal to relieving distress in Ireland would be very limited.

Peel resigned soon after the Corn Laws were repealed, clearing the way for Russell to form (this time successfully) a new Whig government. Politically, Russell was seen as a friend to Ireland. He had worked closely with O'Connell in the 1830s. Nevertheless, wedded to the dogma of *laissez-faire* economics and pulling back on even Peel's limited relief measures, just as a second and much more extensive potato failure was about to hit Ireland in the autumn of 1846, it would be under his government that food shortage turned to famine, a devastating holocaust that in the course of six years saw at least 1 million people die of starvation and related diseases.

The west-coast counties — including Limerick — experienced the worst ravages of the Famine: extensive hunger, destitution and crime. Accounts from Croom spoke of 'emaciated corpses, partly green from eating

211

docks, and partly blue from the cholera and dysentery'. A mill-owner in Shanagolden was assassinated because locals thought he was charging too much for corn. The more prosperous eastern half of County Limerick fared little better, with countless robberies and midnight raids on livestock. In May 1847, for example, 'an armed party with their faces blackened' broke into the home of a farmer named Madigan, near Bruff. They attacked the farmer and his wife with the butts of their guns, and turned the place over in a search for money. The raiders stayed on in the house for more than two hours. They ate bread and veal, and 'regaled themselves' and joked even as blood poured from the heads of their victims, departing at last with bedclothes, jewellery and 'a few shillings'.

Limerick city was spared the worst excesses of the Famine, thanks in part to its famous bacon factories, whose offal provided something of a bulwark against starvation. Food riots were not uncommon, however; a newspaper report in the summer of 1847 detailed how 'a large mob, consisting for the most part of women and boys' attacked several bakers' shops in the city, assaulting the workers with stones and tin cans, and made off with flour and bread. An influx of impoverished rural workers, meanwhile, led to overcrowding in the workhouses and poorer districts of the city — an area vividly described by the novelist William Makepeace Thackeray in 1842 as 'a labyrinth of busy swarming poverty' with every house 'a half ruin' and 'swarming with people'. This crush of people, combined with unsanitary conditions, made Limerick susceptible to contagious diseases, and in spring 1849 it suffered one of the deadliest outbreaks of cholera of the Famine period in the country.

Nothing on this scale, however, could have been even remotely imagined as Douglass stood up at the front of the Independent Chapel on Bedford Row to make his first speech in the city on Monday 10 November 1845.

'Borne on the Wings of the Press'
The venue was 'crowded in all parts . . . by all classes and parties', wrote the *Limerick Reporter*, noting especially the 'large number' of women present. They heard Douglass begin with some familiar references to the 'strange contradiction' of a country boasting to be the 'freest in the world' still harbouring slavery in its 'worst and most aggravated forms'. He mentioned the recent writings of a well-known Scottish geologist, Professor

Charles Lyell, who had returned from a tour of America under the impression 'that the Negro's lot was not an unenviable one'. Lyell, Douglass argued, had been 'taken by the hand by the slaveholding geologists' of the South, walking with their daughters, dining at their tables, staying in their homes. 'It was from these he received all his impressions of slavery, and was it to be presumed that the wolf would say that the lamb loved to be eaten up by him.'

Douglass turned his attention to the imminent admission of Texas into the Union as yet another slave state. America, he said, was not a true democracy, but a 'bastard republicanism'. Not content with enslaving one sixth of its own population, it wanted to go further, stretching its 'long bony fingers into Mexico, and appropriating her territory . . . in order to make it a hotbed of Negro slavery'. Mexico, with all her supposed 'barbarism and darkness', had abolished slavery soon after winning independence from Spain in the 1820s. It took the 'enlightened' and 'Christian' United States, he noted ironically, to stain again what had been 'washed' away. Mixing humour with seriousness in the style advised by *The Columbian Orator* all those years earlier, Douglass then raised cheers with his recollections of events on board the *Cambria*, in particular the part played by the Irish soldier Thomas Gough. Taller even than the six-foot-plus Douglass, Gough had met one of the slaveholder's threats to throw the escaped slave overboard with the reply that 'two might play at that game'.

Douglass next thrilled his audience with the declaration that he wanted Americans to know that he had 'stood up in Limerick and ridiculed their democracy and their liberty'. He wanted his words to reach America, 'borne on the wings of the press beyond the Atlantic waves', so that they could 'fly up and down through the regions of the North . . . cross the line of the slaveholding South . . . reverberate through the valley of the Mississippi'. He ended with a flourish, brandishing once again the iron collar and fetters used to torture slaves, and recalling how his master Thomas Auld had whipped his disabled cousin Henny 'until the blood ran down her back' while quoting from the Bible. The meeting dispersed soon after, although not before some more copies of the Narrative were sold.

During the course of this first talk in Limerick, Douglass also addressed some of the criticisms he had received on his travels, in particular the argument that there were 'white slaves' in Ireland, struggling under the yoke of British oppression, who were much more in need of their countrymen's sympathies than black slaves across the ocean. 'When we are ourselves free,' the *Tipperary Free Press* had editorialised in September, 'let us then engage in any struggle to erase the sin of slavery from every land. But, until then, our own liberation is that for which we should take counsel, and work steadily.'

'But there was nothing like American slavery on the soil on which he now stood,' Douglass retorted strongly, drawing a clear divide between slavery and political oppression. 'Negro slavery consisted not in taking away any of the rights of man, but in annihilating them all — not in taking away a man's property, but in making property of him, and in destroying his identity — in treating him as the beasts and creeping things.' The slave, Douglass continued, was told what to eat, what to drink, what to wear, who to speak to, when to work and even who to marry by his master. 'Could the most inferior person in this country be so treated by the highest?'

This was one of the few times Douglass alluded in any way to Ireland's position under British dominion during the tour. Although inspired by O'Connell, he, unlike Garrison, held back at this stage from even the slightest comment in favour of Repeal. With British support deemed vital to the abolitionist cause, American activists were generally careful not to say anything negative about the country. Douglass, moreover, an avid reader of English authors like Charles Dickens, whose recent *American Notes* contained several searing passages against slavery, was an unabashed Anglophile, his view of Britain still coloured by the emancipation of West Indian slaves, which he always believed to be one of the great moral gestures of the age. And so, while castigating American expansion into Mexico, Douglass 'conveniently overlooked' Britain's own equally regrettable expansion of empire into Asia and Africa, not to mention its long-running struggle to suppress Irish anti-imperial resistance.

Despite the firm riposte to the comments in the *Free Press* and other papers, Douglass was conflicted about pleading the cause of the American slave in a country as impoverished as Ireland, where, indeed, the living quarters of the peasants seemed every bit as horrific as those of his fellow slaves. 'Men and women, married and single, old and young, lie down together, in much the same degradation as of the American slaves,' he wrote to Garrison, echoing a passage from his *Narrative*. 'I see much here to remind me of my former condition, and I confess I should be ashamed to lift up my voice against American slavery, but that I know the cause of humanity is one the world over.'

Douglass may not have talked openly about the devastating scenes of poverty and penury witnessed all over the country during his speeches in Ireland, nevertheless, they made a deep impression, fundamentally altering his world view. 'I am not only an American slave, but a man, and as such, am bound to use my powers for the welfare of the whole human brotherhood,' he would write towards the end of the tour, coming to view his fight against slavery as part of a larger, global struggle against all social injustices. 'I am not going through this land with my eyes shut, ears stopped, or heart steeled. I am seeking to see, hear and feel, all that may be seen, heard and felt . . . I believe that the sooner the wrongs of the whole human family are made known, the sooner those wrongs will be reached.'

'The Disunion Question'

The meeting at the Independent Chapel had been chaired by Benjamin Clark Fisher, a prosperous 63-year-old Quaker linen draper who achieved some minor local celebrity when he introduced the first umbrellas into

Limerick. Douglass also stayed with Fisher at 'Lifford' on the South Circular Road. It was another busy house, with a majority of Fisher's twelve children (eleven daughters and one son) still living at home. One of the daughters, Susanna, seems to have been particularly active in the local anti-slavery group, her name appearing alongside those of 'Miss E. Poole' in Waterford, 'Mrs Allen' in Dublin and 'The Misses Jennings' in Cork on a list of women to whom donations for the Boston Bazaar could be sent, which was attached to the Dublin edition of the *Narrative*. 'If you see Susanna Fisher tell her to write,' Douglass would also ask Webb at a later date. Recently married to Dublin barrister and anti-slavery campaigner Robert Rowan Ross Moore, another daughter, Rebecca, forged a lifelong friendship with the Hutchinson Family after meeting them in the capital.

Douglass also spent time with James J. Fisher, a flour miller and temperance advocate in the city. Although born into a Quaker family, James J., whose wife Lydia (née Leadbetter) was quite friendly with Gerald Griffin, author of the nineteenth-century Irish classic *The Collegians*, had been disowned in the late 1820s for failure to attend Meetings for worship. He appears to have found the Quaker way of life rather sterile. At least he had not been disowned for 'frequenting public houses', dancing, using 'profane' language, carrying arms or involving himself with women of different faiths, as was the case for other Limerick Quakers around this time. Like the Pooles in Wexford and Waterford beforehand, the Fishers in Limerick were all related to Richard D. Webb, either through blood or marriage. Susanna Fisher, indeed, would marry an uncle of Webb's, one of their grandchildren being the economist Ursula Hicks, co-founder of the *Review of Economic Studies* in 1933 and wife of John Hicks, the first British Nobel Prize winner in economics and the most distinguished British economist of his generation. Thomas Fisher, meanwhile, a younger brother of James J. and librarian in Trinity College Dublin, would spend years lodging with his cousin Webb at the house on Great Brunswick Street.

Located at Curragower near the mouth of the River Shannon, James J. Fisher's was just one of a number of important milling companies in the city, Limerick having established itself as the most important milling centre in the south of Ireland. Other prominent millers included Reuben Harvey, James Bannatyne and John Russell, their large operations giving employment to thousands of the labourers and porters who made up the bulk of the city's workforce. Other large industries included the aforementioned bacon-curing businesses, headed by four large companies — Matterson's, Shaw's, O'Mara's and Denny's — all of whom enjoyed worldwide reputations. Lacemaking was another big employer, with 'Limerick Lace' the collective name given to the elaborate and specialised style of hand embroidery practised by numerous lacemakers of the city. Much of the work was carried out in charitable industrial establishments, which was a kind way of describing what were often essentially crowded workhouses for women and children.

Although he stayed for nearly two weeks, Douglass has not left any detailed record of his time in Limerick. It was a small city, however, and we can assume he walked pretty much every inch of its streets, perhaps in the company of Susanna Fisher, one of her sisters or Mary Gough, another Quaker who would write favourably of him to Henry C. Wright. He might have started in the handsome Georgian Quarter before moving down through George's Street (present-day O'Connell Street) where Benjamin Fisher had his shop, to the poorer districts around St Mary's Cathedral and King John's Castle. He would, no doubt, have come across the 'legions' of 'apple-women' who made such a striking impression on Thackeray. 'There were really thousands of them,' wrote the English novelist, 'clustering upon the bridges, squatting down in doorways and vacant sheds for temporary markets, marching and crying their sour goods in all the crowded lanes of the city.' As part of an effort to improve the image of the city a few years later, the local authorities would force all such fruit and vegetable sellers to at least wear shoes.

One of the few surviving letters from his time in Limerick shows Douglass rejecting a suggestion from Webb to combine efforts with Henry C. Wright, the American abolitionist who had spent much of the previous two years touring the British Isles in an effort to generate support for Garrison's quixotic proposal for the anti-slavery states to secede from the Union. In a move seen as another step away from Garrison, he preferred to proceed alone, preaching his own brand of anti-slavery gospel. 'I by no means agree with him [Wright] as to the importance of discussing in this country the disunion question, and I think our difference in this matter would prevent that harmony necessary to success.' Webb was greatly annoyed by Douglass's stance, even though he too had severe doubts about the merit of the so-called 'disunion' campaign.

'*The Plague is Progressing*'
The *Limerick Reporter*, a nationalist paper whose editor John McClenahan would be forced to flee the country in the aftermath of the Young Ireland rebellion, ran an editorial on Douglass a day after his speech at the Independent Chapel. 'There was no man who listened to his eloquent and touching statement that did not burn with indignation against the atrocious system which makes chattel property of men made in the image of God . . . Every word spoken by this persecuted son of Africa bears the impress of truth.' The *Reporter* then turned to the still-contentious question of the Repeal Association and money tainted by slavery, coming down firmly on the side of O'Connell.

In common with our fellow-countrymen, we feel grateful for the sympathy of many Americans in our own struggle for freedom . . . But we trust no slaveholder's polluted dollars ever found their way into the sacred fund of the Repeal Association. If any such dared to make us the medium of his contribution, we would have no hesitation in throwing it in his face, and saying in the language of Peter to Annanias and Sapphira, when they laid a part of their unholy gain at his feet, 'Thy money perish with thee!' Every coin produced by the slave is stained with human blood, and until 'the damned spot' is washed away by abolition of the accursed thing, neither the slaveholder nor his money ought to have part or lot in our glorious struggle for redemption.

The piece on Douglass had been preceded by another long article on the food crisis rapidly enveloping the country. 'The plague is still progressing,' was the stark conclusion. More militant sections of the Repeal movement, led by the Young Irelanders, were already calling for a boycott on paying rent. The *Reporter*, however, was still cautious at this stage, regretting recent violence between tenants and land agents in Castleconnell, a village just outside the city. 'If it is necessary to resort to the extreme measure of keeping the corn and paying no rent,' it declared in true O'Connellite fashion, 'the moral force of public opinion will be quite sufficient for the purpose, and we deprecate all violence as tending to destroy the cause it is designed to serve.'

The *Reporter* did have a couple of issues with Douglass's talk, including his rebuke of a local actor named Bateman for performing in blackface 'Jim Crow . . . apes of the Negro' in city playhouses. 'Mr Bateman is a clever actor,' the paper insisted, 'and his representation of a particular Negro character, debased by his white despot, is no more to be considered as a description of Negroes generally than . . . any of the Irish buffoons represented by [the actors Mr] Leonard or Miss Heron be viewed as types of Irish character.' Minstrel shows, indeed, were a reasonably regular feature of the Victorian stage, whether they were performed by travelling American troupes or British or Irish impersonators. A programme for the Virginia Minstrels show in Dublin in 1844 promised the audience views of the 'sports and pastimes of the Virginia Coloured Race, through the medium of Songs, Refrains and Ditties as sung by Southern slaves'. Despite his annoyance, Douglass would be just as quick to trade in Irish stereotypes, joking to English audiences about the abolitionists adopting the motto of 'Pat, upon entering a Tipperary row' — 'Wherever you see a head, hit it!'

The *Reporter* also disagreed with the choice of location for Douglass's talk, believing it gave a 'sectarian appearance to a cause that equally belongs to all'. With some Catholics hesitant about attending meetings in a Protestant chapel, it wanted any future lectures to be held in a public building accessible to 'the citizens of Limerick at large'. The paper was to be disappointed at first, Douglass returning to the Independent Chapel on Wednesday 12 November for another speech in which he took aim at the Churches in America, especially the Methodists, Presbyterians and Independents, his impression of racist Southern ministers leaving the audience in 'roars of laughter'.

'A Beautiful Sentimental Air'
Douglass's third and final appearance in Limerick came at a large anti-slavery soirée held at the recently built Philosophical Rooms on Glentworth Street — home of the Limerick Philosophical Society — on Friday 21 November. He sat on a raised platform, surrounded by Mayor Francis P. Russell, Catholic priests, Protestant ministers, doctors and prominent businessmen including James J. Fisher. As the St John's Temperance Band played in the background, the mayor toasted (with tea) the health of the evening's guest of honour. Douglass then rose to loud cheers from the more than 400-strong audience, praising the Irish people for having helped free the slaves of the West Indies, but also reminding them that there were more than 3 million slaves in America seeking their

support, crying out 'come and help us'.

This was a shorter, gentler meeting, a celebratory farewell rather than a rallying call. Nevertheless, Douglass still found time to relate how in ports in South Carolina black sailors on foreign-owned ships could be put in jail while their vessels lay in harbour, and sold as slaves if their captains did not collect them. He also likened America's conduct towards Mexico to that of a 'bully', whose only right was 'that of the strongest'. He finished by thanking all those present for their hospitality over the previous two weeks. 'Whether home or abroad he would never forget the very kind manner he was received in Limerick.' The meeting broke up soon after, around eleven o'clock, but not before a number of those present sang some songs. Buoyed by the convivial mood, Douglass joined in, singing 'a beautiful sentimental air', the name of which, unfortunately, is not furnished.

Douglass left for Dublin the next day, before travelling north to Belfast, the last stop on his Irish tour.

10

'The Chattel Becomes a Man'

Belfast was a city on the rise when Frederick Douglass arrived in early December 1845, its thriving port surrounded by linen mills, foundries, warehouses and busy shipbuilding yards. It was also a predominantly Protestant city (although Catholic numbers were increasing) with a deep attachment to the Act of Union. Many local leaders saw prosperity and loyalty as inextricably interlinked. 'Look at the town Belfast,' boasted the Presbyterian minister Henry Cooke. 'When I was a youth it was almost a village. But what a glorious sight it does now present! The masted grove within our harbour — our mighty warehouses teeming with the wealth of every clime — our giant manufactures lifting themselves on every side, and all this we owe to the UNION.' Despite the affluence, there remained deep pockets of poverty, a result, in part, of the city's inability to keep pace with its rapidly growing population. Children as young as nine worked in the mills and entire families, up to a dozen strong, lived in dirty one-room hovels in the poorer parts of the city. The faltering infrastructure, meanwhile, saw sewers flood regularly at high tide, filling low-lying streets with disease-carrying refuse. Nevertheless, the sense was of a city basking in its superiority to the rest of the country, with even the Protestant poor regarding themselves as a sort of 'plebian aristocracy'.

Like many travellers before him, Douglass was quick to note the differences between the industrially vibrant north — where Ballymena, Lurgan, Portadown and Armagh joined Belfast as major textile centres — and the largely agricultural south of the country. 'The north seemed to me far in advance of the south,' he stated quite reasonably. However, Douglass's explanation as to why this should be the case was extremely crude and reductionist. The long-lasting, beneficial effects of Belfast's early adaption to cotton manufacture during the industrial revolution do not get a mention. Nor does Belfast's close proximity to the industrial heartlands of Britain — the north of England and central Scotland. Instead, Douglass blamed religion, food and genes for the south's poverty and apparent backwardness. 'The south is Roman Catholic; its people live mainly on potatoes; and the population is purely Irish . . . no people can be strong and flourish upon a single article of diet . . . In fact, it does not appear that oneness in population, oneness in the matter of religious belief or oneness in diet is favourable to progress.'

Douglass would have been surprised to learn that reliance on the potato was almost as strong in the north as in the south, leading to what Christine Kinealy and Gerard MacAtasney have termed a 'hidden famine' in Belfast a few years later. James Standfield, Maria Webb and other supporters of Douglass during his stay in the city would be heavily involved in the ensuing relief effort.

'Let Them Come'

'Well, all my books went last night at one go,' a delighted Douglass wrote to Richard D. Webb, the day after his first lecture in Belfast, a lecture he had nearly missed owing to snow and ice on the way up from Dublin. 'I want more. I want more. I have everything to hope and nothing to fear. The paper of this morning took a favourable notice of my meeting . . . and a deep interest seems to be excited.'

Held before a crowded Independent Chapel on Donegall Street on Friday 5 December, Douglass's first talk in Belfast began with a standard recapitulation of his life story, from his years as a slave in Maryland to his escape north and the publication of his *Narrative*. It was enlivened with an extended, humorous account of his journey across the Atlantic, the crowd roaring with laughter as Douglass mimicked the slaveholders on board saying 'Oh! I wish I had you in Savannah' and 'Oh! I wish I had you in New Orleans'. For the benefit of the largely Protestant audience, there was a pointed reference to how 'John Bull' — in the person of Captain Judkins of the *Cambria* — had put the slaveholders in their place. Daniel O'Connell was praised for his consistent condemnations of slavery. Nevertheless, conscious of the political beliefs of the majority of his audience, Douglass distanced himself from any support for Repeal. He concluded amidst cheers, imploring the people of Belfast to 'rise up' and 'tell the Americans to tear down their star-spangled banner, and, with its folds, bind up the bleeding wounds of the lacerated slaves'.

As a mark of the esteem in which Douglass was by now held throughout the country, Andrew Mulholland, a wealthy industrialist and Lord Mayor of Belfast in 1845–46, had chaired the meeting. Not everyone, however, was so welcoming, rumours that he was an imposter who had never been a slave accompanying Douglass's arrival in the city. Douglass also had to contend with disgruntled Methodists in Dublin and Cork having sent letters warning their co-religionists about him. Their efforts were in vain: the fair-minded Belfast Methodists opened the doors of their chapels for two of the seven speeches he would make in the city. He was even invited to talk to the children at a Methodist Sabbath School about how he learned to read and write. Douglass seemed happy to accept this opportunity to inculcate some anti-slavery sentiment in the city's youth, although it is not clear if such a talk ever took place.

Webb dispatched another fifty copies of the *Narrative*, but this was quickly dismissed as inadequate. 'I shall probably sell them all on Tuesday night,' Douglass replied, referring to his planned appearance at the Wesleyan Methodist Church. He wanted fifty more, at least, sales of the book so strong he even had the luxury of buying a new watch, 'a right down good one', for £7 10s. 'I swell, but I think I shall not burst.' The letters between Douglass and Webb around this time show relations were still strained. Nevertheless, Douglass promised to take Webb's advice as to being prompter in replying to letters from some of his supporters. There were also touches of kindness: Douglass asked Webb to thank his brother Thomas for the gift of a blanket, which had been 'of great service to me'. In another letter, he wished for a 'speedy deliverance of Mrs Webb and [Webb's son] Richy from their cold'. Douglass had also met and been invited to the home of Maria Webb, a Quaker cousin of his publisher in Belfast. Like so many other members of the family, Maria had been in London for the World Anti-Slavery Convention in 1840, describing William Lloyd Garrison at the time as 'one of God's nobility'. She was just as impressed with Douglass, helping establish a Belfast Ladies Anti-Slavery Society after one of his talks.

Douglass was writing from a comfortable room in the Victoria Hotel on Donegall Street, the city-centre thoroughfare where so many of the churches and meeting houses in which he would lecture were also found. He was entertaining — not entirely happily — a constant stream of visitors. The Belfast Anti-Slavery Society had actually put him up at the hotel instead of someone's home for the express purpose of making him accessible to the public. 'They have gained their purpose thus far . . . everyone that hears me seems to think he has a special claim on my time to listen to his opinion of me, to tell me just how much he condemned and how much he approved. Very well, let them come. I am ready for them though it is not the most agreeable.'

It is no surprise Douglass's visit aroused such strong interest in Belfast, a city with a long history of anti-slavery activity. When the freed slave Olaudah Equiano (like Douglass the author of a famous autobiography) spent eight months lecturing around Ireland in 1791–92, he emphasised how he had been 'particularly' welcomed in Belfast. Equiano had been present when a procession held to celebrate the second anniversary of the fall of the Bastille wound its way through the city, with banners calling for Irish freedom followed by banners denouncing the slave trade. Many of the earliest anti-slavery activists in Belfast, indeed, had been members of the United Irishmen. More recent leaders of the Belfast Anti-Slavery Society continued this tradition of involvement in other causes, albeit of a more philanthropic than political dimension. James Standfield, secretary of the Belfast Anti-Slavery Society at the time of Douglass's visit, was a long-standing member of the Belfast Charitable Society while Lieutenant Francis Calder, who had spent more than a decade with the Royal Navy during the Napoleonic Wars, helped found the Belfast Society for the Prevention of Cruelty to Animals in the 1830s.

The Belfast Anti-Slavery Society had

certainly been active in the years leading up to Douglass's arrival, publishing a large number of pamphlets on different aspects of slavery, including (a favourite topic of Douglass's) the collusion of the American Churches in slavery.

'Send Back the Money'

'Everybody I meet with here seems full of religion, drinks wine and prays,' Douglass half-joked to Webb soon after his arrival in Belfast. But he was also alert to how the intense piety of the city could be turned to advantage in the constant effort to drive a wedge between the British and Irish Churches and their American counterparts. 'The field here is ripe for the harvest; this is the very hotbed of Presbyterianism and Free Churchism, a blow can be struck here more effectually than in any other part of Ireland.' Where previously Douglass's fiercest attacks had been levelled at Methodists, in Belfast his focus turned to the Free Church of Scotland, an evangelical Presbyterian denomination that had recently broken away from the established Church of Scotland. The deep cultural and religious links between Belfast and Scotland ensured a lot of support for the Free Church and, subsequently, disquiet when Douglass condemned it for supporting slavery.

Thomas Chalmers, the Free Church leader, was a deeply moral, intellectual man. Dedicated to alleviating the plight of the urban poor in Scotland, he had also written a pamphlet criticising slavery in the 1820s. Nevertheless, when the newly established Free Church embarked on a fundraising campaign among Presbyterians in America, he had no hesitation accepting thousands of dollars in donations from slaveholding states. 'I do not need to assure you how little I sympathise with those who — because slavery happens to prevail in the Southern States of America — would unchristianise that whole region,' he informed a correspondent. American abolitionists were outraged. Chalmers responded in a formal letter stating: 'Slavery, like war, is a great evil . . . Yet destructive and demoralising as both are . . . it follows not that there may not be a Christian soldier, and neither does it follow that there may not be a Christian slaveholder.'

The Belfast Anti-Slavery Society published Chalmers' letter as a penny pamphlet, with refutations in the margins. Douglass, too, was unconvinced, labelling Chalmers an 'apologist' for slavery at talks held on successive nights at the Rev. Samuel Hanna's Presbyterian Meeting House on 11 and 12 December. He renewed his attack on the Free Church two nights before Christmas, having left Belfast briefly for a talk in Birmingham organised by John Cadbury, the philanthropic founder of the chocolate empire. Placards announcing Douglass's return to the city publicised the meeting in advance.

'Ladies and gentlemen, one of the most painful duties I have been called on to perform in the advocacy of the Abolition of Slavery, has been to expose the corruption and sinful position of the American Churches with regard to that question,' Douglass began, the Independent Chapel once again filled to excess. Nevertheless, the behaviour of these Churches and their ministers compelled him to do so, the only way of 'purifying our church from the deep damnation into which she was plunging' being to 'expose her deeds to the light'. And so, Douglass assailed the Baptists and Congregationalists in America for almost an hour, exposing distinguished clergymen by name as 'women-whippers', 'cradle-plunderers' and 'man-stealers'.

'Slaveholders!' Douglass continued impassionedly, 'Oh, my friends, do not rank the slaveholders as a common criminal — as no worse than a sheep-stealer or a horse-stealer. The slaveholder is not only a thiever of men, but he is a murderer; not a murderer of the body, but, what is infinitely worse, a murderer of the soul — (hear, hear, hear) — as far as a man can murder the soul of his fellow-creature, for he shuts out the light of salvation from his spirit.' He then held up a newspaper clipping and read aloud the announcement of the auction of the estate of a Baptist clergyman Richard Furman (*The Columbian Orator* had long ago placed a premium on such gestures). For sale was land 'together with twenty-seven Negroes — *some of them very fine* — a library *chiefly theological* — *two mules* and *an old wagon*'. The audience laughed; Douglass did not. 'We should be sadly weeping to think that such a man ever lived.'

At last, Douglass turned his attention to the Free Church, imploring it to 'send back the blood-stained money' and have 'no communion with the American slaveholders'. The 'blood of the slave', he said, 'forbade' the American Churches such fellowship, and if the Free Church and all the other Churches on the British Isles only heeded his call, they would give slavery 'a blow under which it would stagger'.

This speech has been described as 'one of the great emotional triumphs' of Douglass's life. It certainly made an impact in Belfast, with some papers curtailing their coverage and leaving out the passages unfavourable to the Free Church. A number of the leading clergymen in the city had actually absented themselves from the meeting, in light of Douglass's earlier denunciations of Chalmers. There was also a dispute among pro- and anti-Douglass papers, the *Northern Whig* and the *Banner of Ulster*, as to whether or not the chair of the meeting, James Gibson, had intervened to distance himself from Douglass's harsh comments. The two papers would still be quarrelling about the Free Church long after Douglass left the city.

Douglass's uncompromising tone may have alienated some important evangelical reformers in Belfast, but it also won new adherents to the anti-slavery cause. Writing to Maria Weston Chapman a few weeks after his departure, Mary Ireland, a teacher at the Belfast Academical Institution, described how an 'intense interest' had been 'excited' by Douglass's oratory, and that there was 'scarcely a lady in Belfast who would not be anxious to join in any means calculated to promote the enfranchisement of the deeply injured Africans'. A woman named Mary Cunningham, meanwhile, was writing incredulously to an old childhood friend, Thomas Smyth, a Lurgan-born Presbyterian minister in South Carolina who was closely associated with Chalmers and the Free Church. 'I must now tell you to what subject my attention has been lately directed, that of 'Slavery', from the eloquent and affecting lectures addressed to the inhabitants of this town by a Fugitive Slave. I never before knew the heart-sickening horrors of this dreadful system . . . I have learned, with deep regret, that *slaveholders* are admitted to Communion in several churches of the United States, and that even *Ministers of 'The Gospel'* hold their fellow creatures in this state of frightful bondage. O! can such things be?'

Moreover, Douglass had hit upon the evocative slogan — 'Send back the money' — that would carry him through Scotland in the early months of 1846, when he finally left Ireland to start a tour of mainland Britain that would last until the spring of 1847.

'Send Back the Nigger'
Douglass sailed to Scotland in early January 1846, having being feted at a public breakfast chaired by William Sharman Crawford MP and attended by clergymen from all over Ulster. He carried a beautiful new Bible across the Irish Sea, a 'golden gift', as he called it, from the Belfast Anti-Slavery Society (to go along with the £200 they raised for him). Presented by the Presbyterian clergyman the Rev. Isaac Nelson, one of his

strongest supporters during his time in the city and later a prominent Home Rule MP, a lengthy inscription on the first page assured Douglass of the Society's 'respect and esteem' for his 'personal character' and urged him to continue to expose 'by the torch of Divine truth' all who attempted to 'defend or palliate slavery'. There was, however, a litigious coda to Douglass's time in Belfast.

After six months' successful travelling, lecturing and agitating across Scotland and the north of England, Douglass returned to Belfast for a couple of weeks in July, at the same time as the annual Presbyterian Assembly was being held in the city. Also present was the aforementioned Rev. Dr Thomas Smyth of Charleston, South Carolina (the staunch defender of slavery had returned home to deal with some matters relating to an inheritance). Anti-slavery sentiment was still strong, Isaac Nelson urging the Assembly to break fraternal relations with their American brethren. Smyth, indeed, found the city in a complete 'hub-bub' about Douglass, and instead of being welcomed into the Assembly as an honoured visitor, as would ordinarily have been case, was actually shut out when he tried to gain admittance.

A few days later, Douglass, Standfield and Nelson presided over an anti-slavery rally at the seaside town of Bangor, County Down, the latter exulting that American Presbyterians would learn by the 'exclusion' of Smyth 'that even when a native of our own town of Belfast becomes untrue to the great cause of freedom, we, as Churches, are determined, by refusing him admission to our Assembly, to settle ... our fixed resolve to have no fellowship with slave-holders'. Hurt and angered by the manner in which he had been received, Smyth spread a rumour that Douglass had been seen leaving a brothel in Manchester, a monumentally damaging slur in a city as pious as Belfast. 'Send Back the Nigger' placards appeared on the streets, Webb informed Chapman, posted either by Smyth himself or some supporters.

Members of the Belfast Anti-Slavery Societyconfronted Smyth, with Robert Jackson Bell, another old school friend of Smyth, acting as a conduit for letters between Douglass and the Presbyterian minister. (Their friendship, Bell wrote sadly, was at an end.) When nothing came from these meetings and communications, Douglass (guided no doubt by his Belfast friends) engaged legal representation. On 16 July, Douglass's solicitors, Davison and Torrens, notified Smyth that unless some satisfactory explanation was forthcoming a libel action would be commenced. The affair clearly affected Douglass, and he blamed 'the foul slanders of this Rev man-stealer' when apologising to Isabel Jennings for being somewhat abrupt in a letter to her. Nevertheless, after a couple more weeks of procrastination, Smyth finally signed an apology that expressed 'sincere regret for having uttered' statements 'injurious' to Douglass's 'moral and religious character', which statements were 'incautiously made, on the report of third parties'. It was published in *The Liberator* and other papers.

Douglass was back in England by the time the apology was made, speaking to crowds of thousands all over the country, dining with statesmen, meeting with editors and even contemplating moving his family over permanently. The great success of this leg of the tour, combined with continued sales of his *Narrative* (30,000 copies sold by 1850 and French, Dutch and German translations all coming into print), ensured Douglass returned to America in April 1847 a celebrity and icon of international standing. He was also, much more importantly, a free man, a group of anti-slavery campaigners in Newcastle making contact with the Aulds in late 1846 and raising the £150 (just over $700 at the time) needed to secure his manumission. There was

a great deal of criticism of the move, abolitionists like Henry C. Wright believing it amounted
to trafficking with slaveholders and dimin-
ished Douglass's (and the movement's) moral
power. Douglass, however, supported by
William Lloyd Garrison among others, preferred to be a free anti-slavery worker rather
than a martyr.

The woman who instigated the negotia-
tions to purchase Douglass's official freedom
was Anna Richardson (née Atkins), sister of
Ann Jennings of Cork, aunt to Douglass's
'Dear Isa'.

'Behold the Change'

'I am now about to take leave of the Emerald
Isle, for Glasgow, Scotland,' Douglass wrote
to Garrison on 1 January 1846, unaware that
he would be back for brief visits in July and
October. He was in a reflective mood, having
enjoyed 'some of the happiest moments' of
his life since landing in the country. 'I seem to
have undergone a transformation. I live a new
life.' He continued:

The warm and generous co-operation
extended to me by the friends of my despised
race, the prompt and liberal manner with
which the press has rendered me its aid

— the glorious enthusiasm with which thousands have flocked to hear the cruel wrongs of my downtrodden and long-enslaved fellow-countrymen portrayed — the deep sympathy for the slave, and the strong abhorrence of the slaveholder, everywhere evinced — the cordiality with which members and ministers of various religious bodies, and of various shades of religious opinion, have embraced me, and lent me their aid — the kind hospitality constantly proffered to me by persons of the highest rank in society — the spirit of freedom that seems to animate all with whom I come into contact — and the entire absence of everything that looked like prejudice against me, on account of the colour of my skin — contrasted so strongly with my long and bitter experience in the United States, that I look with wonder and amazement on the transition.

Douglass had been away from America for four and a half months, and although there were times when he thought fondly of her 'bright blue sky . . . grand old woods . . . fertile fields . . . beautiful rivers . . . mighty lakes . . . and star-crowned mountains', such reveries never lasted very long, the escaped slave remembering how 'with the waters of her noblest rivers', the tears of his 'brethren' were 'borne to the ocean', while her 'most fertile fields' drank daily 'of the warm blood of my outraged sisters'. In the South, Douglass wrote, he had been a slave, 'thought of and spoken of as property'; in the North, a fugitive slave, 'liable to be hunted at any moment like a felon, and to be hurled [back] into the terrible jaws of slavery'. 'But now behold the change!' he exclaimed. 'Eleven days and a half gone, and I have crossed three thousand miles of the perilous deep. Instead of a democratic government, I am under a monarchical government. Instead of the bright blue sky of America, I am covered with the soft grey fog of the Emerald Isle. I breathe, and lo! the chattel becomes a man.'

Encouraged and applauded almost every step of the way, Douglass would always consider his time in Ireland a transformative experience, a milestone in his personal and political development. He grew much more confident and began to follow his own path — free from the dictates and demands of the American Anti-Slavery Society leadership. This included engagement in the political process and even — something his Irish hero O'Connell would have opposed as much as Garrison — the forging of alliances with violent radicals like John Brown, hanged after a failed attempt to start a slave insurrection in Virginia in 1859. (Brown would later be the subject of a biography by Webb as well as a poem by his daughter Deborah.) The clearest manifestation of this new independence of mind was Douglass's decision to move his family away from the Garrisonian enclave of Boston to the smaller town of Rochester in upstate New York a few months after he returned to America. He set up a newspaper, the *North Star*, in part with funds raised by Isabel Jennings and Maria Webb. This was succeeded a few years later by *Frederick Douglass's Paper*, in whose pages he would relentlessly attack slavery during the tumultuous decade leading up to the American Civil War, becoming in the process the most formidable black leader in a country of almost 4 million slaves. The war itself would see him advise President Abraham Lincoln at the White House and help recruit men for the famous 54th Massachusetts Infantry Regiment, the black unit of which two of his own sons were members.

Inspired by O'Connell and deeply affected by the scenes of poverty that shadowed him all over the country, the changes wrought by Ireland went further still, for it was during this tour that the great humanitarian Douglass was born. Where previously his focus had been purely on anti-slavery, he increasingly turned his attention to the 'wrongs and sufferings' of the 'great family of man', speaking out, for example, in support of Europe's oppressed masses during the 'Year of Revolutions' in 1848. He also attended the world's first Women's Rights Convention in Seneca Falls, New York, that year, remaining a dedicated suffragist all his life. Subsequent years would see Douglass lend his weighty voice and influence to campaigns for free public education, prison reform and the abolition of capital punishment — 'Murder is no cure for murder'. Late in life, having served two years as the American Minister and Consul-General on the island, Douglass would devote a lot of time and energy to helping Haiti, a country that, as the first black Republic in the world, following a successful slave uprising against Napoleonic rule, always meant a great deal to African Americans. He became the 'broadhearted humanitarian' he saw in O'Connell.

'It's a Miserable Country'
Douglass may have been transformed by his time in Ireland, but what impact did he have on the country? The tour was certainly a success, the forty or so speeches delivered

and thousands of copies of the *Narrative* sold raising great awareness of the anti-slavery cause. He was the catalyst for the formation of a new anti-slavery society in Belfast and for new members joining existing groups around the country. 'There never was a person who made a greater sensation in Cork,' wrote Isabel Jennings. 'He has gained friends everywhere he has been.'

The campaign against the American Churches also paid some dividends, with Belfast Baptists and Independents sending anti-slavery addresses to their co-religionists in America after hearing him speak. Inspired by Douglass's talks, some Dublin Methodists told Webb that they, too, would push their Church to do more on the issue. The Free Church of Scotland never sent back the 'blood-stained' money; nevertheless, its leaders had to contend with the formation of a Free Church Anti-Slavery Society, uncomfortable questioning at their next General Assembly and a storm of public opprobrium. Stoked up by Douglass and others, the tensions between the Churches on the two sides of the Atlantic were clearly evident at the Evangelical Alliance, a meeting of primarily British and American evangelical religions like Baptists and Methodists held in London in August 1846. With giant abolitionist rallies taking place outside, arguments about slavery dominated discussions; the British section of the meeting refused membership to slaveholding ministers.

A particularly tangible measure of Douglass's success was the increase in donations for the Boston Bazaar. 'We think we have got contributions from persons belonging to the [established] Church [of England] who never could have been influenced except by a person who had himself suffered,' Isabel Jennings informed Maria Weston Chapman in late 1845. A year later, a still embittered Webb was forced to admit: 'There can be no doubt that much of the sweep of the Bazaar this year may be attributed to him [Douglass] — for from all I can learn the contributions from this side of the Atlantic will be finer than ever.'

Despite these apparent gains, the thousands-strong meetings in Dublin and other large gatherings across the country did not turn the anti-slavery campaign into a broader mass movement in Ireland. This would probably have been the case even if those most closely connected with the cause had not been forced almost immediately to shift their attention away from the plight of the slaves and onto the victims of the worsening Famine. Led by Maria Webb, the Belfast Ladies Anti-Slavery Society turned all its efforts into the Belfast

Ladies Association for the Relief of Irish Distress. In Dublin, James Haughton became ever more deeply involved in the various charities he supported. He also wrote public letters advocating the shutting down of breweries and distilleries to save grain. On a practical level, as a corn merchant, he stopped trading in malt and barley. Richard Allen and Webb, meanwhile, joined the Central Relief Committee of the Society of Friends, the body established in late 1846 on the suggestion of Joseph Bewley (the tea and coffee merchant whose name still adorns several well-known cafes in Dublin) to raise funds, organise relief measures and distribute supplies; Webb also travelled to the most deprived areas of Galway and Mayo to compile first-hand accounts of the distress for the committee.

As a body, the Quakers would play a hugely important role in relief efforts during the Famine, setting up a network of soup kitchens across the country and distributing money, food, clothing and blankets to individuals and local relief committees. Trusted with funds from donors of all religious persuasions, they were particularly successful at raising money in the United States and Canada, including from Garrison and the American Anti-Slavery Society. Completely independent of the government whose measures they criticised, they were also scrupulously impartial in whom they helped, avoiding the accusation of 'souperism' — aid contingent upon religious conversion — levelled at other Protestant charity and relief efforts. With at least fifteen members dying after contracting diseases from those they were helping, the immense efforts of the Quakers during the Famine are lauded to this day. Nevertheless, there were some moments of controversy, such as when Webb and Allen argued (unsuccessfully) for the rejection of donations sent from the slave states of Maryland and South Carolina.

From Cork, Isabel Jennings, involved like so many other anti-slavery activists in the distribution of food to the poorest quarters of the city, described the effects of the Famine to Maria Weston Chapman, albeit not in a manner that shows her in an entirely favourable light. 'We have seen the children lying dead in their mother's arms,' she wrote of the (mainly Catholic) peasants coming into the city from towns like Skibbereen in the west of the county. But even before the Famine large numbers of these poor country people had died of want. 'This did not prevent the people marrying nor did it cause them to lay by anything for the future — all they cared for was enough of potatoes,' she noted superiorly. 'When they came into Cork you knew they were human beings but so very low in the scale that you could not *feel* they were your brethren. This may be wrong but if we had known them even to care for any intellectual enjoyment we w[oul]d have been a thousand times more unhappy at their fate.'

Against this backdrop of famine and suffering, the anti-slavery movement in Ireland fell away during the late 1840s, Webb not even bothering to circulate appeals for the Boston Bazaar outside his immediate circle, so 'frightful' was the extent of 'poverty and pauperism' in the country. 'I tell you, it's a miserable country for a man to be in, and I would be heartily glad to be well out of it,' he would write Maria Weston Chapman in 1847, the worst year of the Famine. Two years later, he derided the idea of holding an anti-slavery bazaar in Ireland. It would be looked on as a piece of 'philanthropic knight errantry' and should be abandoned.

In the years that followed, black and white American abolitionists, including Charles Lenox Remond's sister, Sarah, continued to tour Ireland as part of trips to Great Britain or Europe. Wider interest in the cause also flared up occasionally, for instance after the publication of Douglass's friend Harriet

Beecher Stowe's famous anti-slavery novel *Uncle Tom's Cabin* in the early 1850s. Nevertheless, by the time of the American Civil War and Abraham Lincoln's Emancipation Proclamation, the anti-slavery scene in Ireland still centred on the same small coterie of Quakers and Unitarians: the Webbs, the Allens and the Haughtons.

Ireland, it seems, had far greater impact on Douglass than the celebrated ex-slave had on the country.

Epilogue

Queenstown — 1886

Frederick Douglass did see Ireland again, at either end of a tour of Europe and Africa in the late 1880s. Sailing from America on board the luxury steamer the *City of Rome* with his second wife Helen Pitts Douglass, Anna having died four years earlier, he skirted the mountainous south coast of the country in September 1886, stopping in Queenstown (Cobh) for a couple of hours. 'Poor, barefooted Ireland!' he exclaimed, gazing sadly upon the shore he had first set foot on four decades earlier.

The years between had seen the fugitive slave transform into a statesman, writer and orator of world renown, a friend of presidents and the most prominent anti-slavery campaigner of the age. Ireland, however, had never strayed far from his mind — if not always for positive reasons. He certainly had sympathy for the plight of the hundreds of thousands of Irish people forced to leave the country during the Famine, writing movingly of how they must have felt on board the ships carrying them to America, Canada and Australia. 'Not even the comforting thought of going to a better and happier country can dispel the bitter anguish of an Irish emigrant, when he sees one after another of the familiar hills and mountains of his beloved native land sink below the distant horizon. It is a moment when strong hearts fail and nature speaks in tears.' He also spoke passionately about the country during the tumultuous 'Year of Revolutions' in 1848, using much stronger language than ever before. 'Ireland, ever chafing under oppressive rule, famine-stricken, ragged and wretched, but warm-hearted, generous and unconquerable Ireland, caught up the inspiring peal . . . and again renewed her oath, to be free or die. Her cause is already sanctified by the martyrdom of [the transported Young Irelander John] Mitchel, and millions stand ready to be sacrificed in the same manner.'

Douglass would not remain so sympathetic for long, regretting that Daniel O'Connell had been succeeded 'by the Duffys, Mitchels, Meaghers and others — men who loved liberty for themselves and their country, but were utterly destitute of sympathy with the cause of liberty in countries other than their own'. He was particularly disgusted with Mitchel, who became an apologist for slavery in his New York newspaper *The Citizen* after escaping the penal colony of Van Diemen's Land (Tasmania) for America in the early 1850s. There were deeper currents to Mitchel's thinking than pure racism, including a real abhorrence of the industrial capitalist system of the North as opposed to the largely agrarian South. Nevertheless, it is hard to find any nuance in his wish for 'a good plantation, well-stocked with healthy Negroes in Alabama', a riposte to James Haughton's forlorn call on the Young Ireland exiles in America to condemn slavery.

Douglass was just as disappointed in the broader mass of Famine emigrants flocking to New York and other east coast cities. 'The Irish, who, at home, readily sympathise with the oppressed everywhere, are instantly taught when they step upon our soil to hate and despise the Negro,' he wrote. 'They are taught to believe that he eats the bread that belongs to them.' Empathy gave way to anger, Douglass turning on 'Pat, fresh from the Emerald Isle, requiring two sober men to keep him on his legs, enter and deposit his vote for the Democratic candidate amid the loud hurrahs of his fellow citizens.'

Tensions between Irish Americans and African Americans reached a murderous nadir during the New York draft riots of 1863, Irish mobs attacking innocent blacks on streets. 'There is perhaps no darker chapter in the whole history of the war than this cowardly and bloody uprising, in July, 1863,' Douglass wrote.

For three days and nights New York was in the hands of a ferocious mob, and there was not sufficient power in the government of the country or of the city itself to stay the hand of violence and the effusion of blood. Though this mob was nominally against the draft which had been ordered, it poured out its fiercest wrath upon the coloured people and their friends. It spared neither age nor sex; it hanged Negroes simply because they were Negroes; it murdered women in their homes, and burnt their homes over their heads; it dashed out the brains of young children against the lampposts; it burned the coloured orphan asylum . . . and, scarce allowing time for the helpless 200 children to make good their escape, plundered the building of every valuable piece of furniture; and forced colored men, women and children to seek concealment in cellars or garrets or wheresoever else it could be found, until this high carnival of crime and reign of terror should pass away.

Douglass's account was exaggerated — but only just. And yet he never fully lost faith in Ireland and the Irish, making a number of speeches in favour of Home Rule in the 1880s.

Much more important than any political speeches or newspaper articles were the letters that kept Douglass in touch with friends from Ireland, those exchanged with Isabel Jennings, in particular, generally full of warmth and honesty, 'My love to all at Brown Street' the regular refrain.

Douglass was also in contact with Richard D. Webb quite a lot for a few years after he left Ireland, albeit largely on account of new editions of *Narrative of the Life of Frederick Douglass, an American Slave* rather than any mutual regard. The two men, in fact, were still bickering over the portrait used for the second Dublin edition of the book — published in 1846 — as late as 1864. Webb's letters to Maria Weston Chapman and other Garrisonians, meanwhile, were regularly filled with caustic complaints about Maria Webb in Belfast, the Jennings sisters in Cork and many other female activists in Ireland believing the whole anti-slavery cause was bound up in Douglass. He also complained about them sending material to the Rochester Bazaar instead of Boston. Nevertheless, the publisher was able to admit some of Douglass's good aspects, including his talents as a writer and honesty about money. Douglass was also among the recipients of a letter Webb sent to friends in America after the death of his wife Hannah in 1862.

Douglass, for his part, would be very welcoming to Webb's son Richard junior when he visited America in 1859, apologising, indeed, for some harsh words he had recently written about Webb in his newspaper. Alfred Webb would be just as warmly received when he travelled across the Atlantic in the early 1870s. (Alfred, eight years old in 1845 but now a prominent Home Ruler, also met William Lloyd Garrison, James Buffum and Charles Lenox Remond on this trip, all of whom spoke warmly of his father.) Douglass would continue to open his door to an array of Irish visitors in the years that followed, from Maria Webb's son Richard (yet another Richard Webb) to Rebecca Moore, one of the Benjamin Clarke Fisher's eleven daughters from Limerick, and Lydia Shackleton, a well-known painter and member of the famous Ballitore Quaker dynasty.

Douglass's most intimate Irish correspondence in later years was with Richard Allen, who still had a drapery business in Dublin. Allen had travelled to America with his second wife, Mary Ann Savage, in 1883, his first wife, Ann, having died in 1868. A month spent in the South made an especially deep impression on the old anti-slavery campaigner. He spoke at schools, attended black churches and looked over cotton fields in visits arranged by fellow Quakers. 'My heart did feel stirred at seeing such a number of coloured people *all free*,' wrote Allen, by now in his eighties, after attending morning prayers at a school in Memphis, Tennessee. At Fisk University in Nashville, meanwhile, Allen's wife noticed a print of Benjamin Haydon's famous painting of the World Anti-Slavery Convention hanging up in a room, bringing the Principal's attention to the fact that her husband was one of the figures depicted. They met Douglass in Washington — 'My Dear Richard Allen: Can it be that you are still alive and, more wonderful still, in America? I could hardly believe my own eyes when I read your note this morning' — where they spent hours talking about old friends and the chequered progress of African Americans since Emancipation. Douglass had moved to Washington in 1872, and at the time of Allen's visit was Recorder of Deeds for the District of Columbia, one of a number of government positions he would hold in the years following the Civil War.

The renewal of this friendship of some forty years' standing was followed by a flow of letters across the Atlantic. 'My Dear Friend,' Douglass wrote, 'I am obliged for your letter . . . It brought Brooklawn quite near me, and I could see yourself and Mrs Allen comfortably seated at your warm fireside. What a blessing this mail service between friendly souls is! How good that we can speak to each other over the wide waste of waters!' Allen, always happy to relive memories of his 'American ramble', con- gratulated Douglass on his marriage to Helen, his secretary while Recorder of Deeds in Washington. Douglass was in his late sixties when they married, Helen in her late forties. The twenty-year age difference, however, was much less controversial than the fact that Helen was a white woman. Douglass appreciated Allen's warm words when so many others, including his daughter Rosetta, had been harsh. 'My marriage has brought to me clouds and darkness and strong criticism for offending popular prejudice, but there is peace and happiness within. I was unwilling to allow the world to select a wife for me, but preferred to select for myself, and the world is deplored with my independence.'

Douglass also raised the possibility of a visit to Ireland. 'It has long been my desire to look once more upon Ireland and to see some of the warm-hearted and generous friends who greeted me there forty years ago.' He worried, however, that any such trip would bring more sadness than joy, the majority of his friends from his first visit having passed away. Webb and Haughton, for example, had died within a year of each other, in July 1872 and March 1873 respectively. Allen, too, was in poor health, admitting that at eighty-three years of age he could look for nothing beyond 'temporary improvement'. He died a few months after writing this letter, in January 1886. A note on his death found in Douglass's private papers described how Allen was still talking about the old anti-slavery days to visitors while confined to his bed, recalling especially the presentation of the women's anti-slavery address to Queen Victoria in 1837.

Despite these reservations, Douglass did visit Ireland again, stopping off in Dublin for about a week in July 1887, at the end of a year-long holiday that had taken in Britain, France, Italy, Greece and Egypt. He travelled on his own, Helen having just returned to America to care for her ailing mother. It was a slightly strange but nonetheless fulfilling experience, Douglass surrounded for the most part by the children of his old friends rather than the friends themselves. He stayed with Maria Webb's daughter, Wilhelmina, in Killiney, County Dublin, one of her letters giving him the days on which the Bristol steamer crossed directly to Dublin and also the times of the trains from the city to her house. If he got the mail boat to Kingstown (Dun Laoghaire), she would meet him at the dock. Wilhelmina had actually been corresponding with Douglass for a couple of years. 'Although this is the first time that I have addressed you by letter, my name may not be unfamiliar to you as the daughter of William and Maria Webb,' she had written in January 1885, adding that she had a 'very distinct remembrance' of him from when he had visited their house in Belfast. She had hoped Douglass would write a few words about her recently deceased mother for a memorial her sister Anna was putting together. Douglass happily obliged.

In another letter, Wilhelmina told Douglass how her husband, John, had been working as an apprentice in Limerick in 1845 and had met him several times at Benjamin Clarke Fisher's home. She also described how happy Richard Allen had been to read over some of the letters Douglass had sent her just before he died. Wilhelmina and Douglass continued to write to each other after he returned to

America. Douglass sent press cuttings with little notes; Wilhelmina wrote mainly about family matters, the endless cycle of births, marriages and deaths, as well as that age-old Irish obsession — the weather. She also sent a photograph of herself and her husband as a Christmas present in 1887. Deborah Webb, on the other hand, would write thanking Douglass for a photograph he sent back of himself, everyone taking advantage of the advances in photographic technology — the first Kodak camera had come onto the market around this time.

Douglass also spent some time with Wilhelmina's sister, Anna Webb Shackleton, during his stay in Dublin, remembering the lines she had written as a precocious twelve-year-old just as he was about to leave Belfast: 'Oh then depart if it will spread the cause / Of justice, liberty and righteous laws.' Henry and Hannah Wigham, Wilhelmina's close neighbours in Killiney, were another family to see a good deal of the famous visitor. The Wighams were a well-known Quaker clan, some of whom Douglass had met in Scotland in 1846. Hannah was a writer and Douglass had been impressed with her recently published biography of Richard Allen. She promised him a signed copy, together with a book on John Woolman, the eighteenth-century American Quaker and anti-slavery campaigner, with a few particularly 'prophetic' passages underlined. Lydia Shackleton, the artist, meanwhile, would send him a painting of Bray Head after he went home, together with a 'handful' of heather and furze from Howth Head — surely one of the stranger gifts to cross the Atlantic — so that Douglass would always have a bit of Ireland.

While appreciative of the kindness and hospitality of Wilhelmina Webb and her friends, it is not hard to imagine Douglass's reunion with Susanna Fisher, the sister to whom he had been closest in Limerick, carrying a much deeper emotional resonance. She had married a Webb in the 1850s and now lived in Dublin. 'Sometimes it seems more like a dream than reality that you have been here — and we have really and truly seen you again — and not so very much changed at all,' she wrote the following summer. 'The hair white certainly and the figure stouter and less active but the same spirit of the man.' She, too, had been writing to thank him for a photograph he had sent over, which we can assume took pride of place on the mantelpiece or wall of her tidy Rathmines home.

Douglass did not make it out of Dublin on this visit. Nevertheless, his brief sojourn in the city was the signal for renewed contact with Isabel Jennings in Cork. There was still a great deal of affection in the letters, even if Isabel's news was not particularly happy. 'But you may not know that only three of the large family in Brown Street now remain in this region, called 'The World,'' she wrote, giving the dates for the deaths of her parents and siblings. She had had problems with cataracts but was now 'wonderfully recovered'. Nevertheless, at seventy-four, she said she looked on death as a 'dear friend', although to 'the dear, loving Father I leave the time'. Douglass, too, was increasingly aware of his own mortality. Writing to Richard Allen a few years earlier on the possibility of returning to Ireland he had suggested that while there were a good many people whose hand he would like to shake again, it did not matter if he did it in this world or the next — 'It will not be long before we all meet on the other shore.'

Douglass died on the evening of 20 February 1895, having just returned home from a women's rights rally. He was buried four days later, the elderly John W. Hutchinson, one of his fellow travellers on that first great trip to Ireland, singing over the grave. Douglass was seventy-seven years old, even if his gravestone added a year, the uncertainty sown by slavery taking physical form. He had died a rich man, passing away in one of the twenty-one rooms in his huge Cedar Hill home, perched high on a hilltop with a sweeping view of Washington, D.C. The wealth and garlands, however, had never fully dimmed his radical spirit. Blacks were free but they were not equal and Douglass had spent the last decades of his life fighting the segregation laws that slowly but surely spread through the South. And so it was that when a young man visited his home a few years before his death and asked for advice, Douglass's answer — lifted straight from the lips of his hero O'Connell — was: 'Agitate! Agitate! Agitate!'

Acknowledgements

I have been very lucky in the writing of this book to have online access to a great wealth of Frederick Douglass and anti-slavery material from some of the most important libraries in the United States, in particular the Library of Congress, Boston Public Library, Stanford, Cornell and Yale.

Closer to home, I would like to thank Mary Shackleton for permission to quote from some correspondence in her possession, Christopher Moriarty of the Quaker Historical Library in Dublin and Richard S. Harrison, Quaker historian extraordinaire. Thanks, too, to Brian McGee and Timmy O'Connor at the Cork City and County Archives, the staff of the Special Collections, University College Cork and all at The Collins Press.

We do hope that you have enjoyed reading this large print book.

Did you know that all of our titles are available for purchase?

We publish a wide range of high quality large print books including:
Romances, Mysteries, Classics
General Fiction
Non Fiction and Westerns

Special interest titles available in large print are:
The Little Oxford Dictionary
Music Book
Song Book
Hymn Book
Service Book

Also available from us courtesy of Oxford University Press:
Young Readers' Dictionary
(large print edition)
Young Readers' Thesaurus
(large print edition)

For further information or a free brochure, please contact us at:
Ulverscroft Large Print Books Ltd.,
The Green, Bradgate Road, Anstey,
Leicester, LE7 7FU, England.
Tel: (00 44) 0116 236 4325
Fax: (00 44) 0116 234 0205